A LITTLE A DAY KEEPS
THE DOG TRAINER AWAY

A Little a Day Keeps the Dog Trainer Away

A Beginner's Guide to Raising a Happy and Obedient Dog

Tom Roderick

LIONCREST
PUBLISHING

A LITTLE A DAY KEEPS THE DOG TRAINER AWAY

A Beginner's Guide to Raising a Happy and Obedient Dog

ISBN   978-1-61961-637-0 *Paperback*

978-1-61961-638-7 *Ebook*

Over the course of my career, I've come to realize that the craft of training dogs will always be an evolution. It has become a lifelong commitment for me to continue to discover new and exciting ways to motivate our canines in the most effective ways possible.

Since 2005 I have bettered my training and, in turn, been able to help more and more owner/dog relationships meet their fullest potential. It is with this in mind that I would like to dedicate this book to all of the dogs I've been lucky enough to work with and who have helped me get to the level of success at which I gratefully find myself today.

So, here's to you, my wonderful canine friends!

Contents

For the sake of simplicity, throughout the book I have referred to all dogs as females. The training, of course, is equally applicable to both sexes.

Introduction

Why Train Your Dog?

THE POWER OF TRAINING

I've always gravitated towards animals, particularly dogs. They're more accessible than other domestic creatures or wild animals, and that makes it easy to be near them, interact with them, and pet them.

As a child, I often visited my grandfather's estate in Ligonier, Pennsylvania. He kept Jack Russells and black Labradors. The Labradors were working dogs, and the Jack Russells had free run of the house. I soon learned the difference between a trained dog and an untrained dog.

One day, I was wrestling on the ground with my little brother, and one of the Jack Russells ran straight out of left field and attacked me. This was a dog that got away with murder. She barked out of the windows, behaved extremely dominantly towards other dogs, was allowed up on the couch whenever she wanted, was never crated, and once snacked on the mailman's boots, for which she was never punished.

The Labradors were completely different. My grandfather used them to retrieve birds, so they were used to holding things very gently in their mouths. Jim, their trainer, encouraged me to put my arm into the kennel. I was only nine years old, and I was scared. "No, I don't want to do it," I said. "It'll bite me," but Jim convinced me.

The dog's name was Annie. When I got up the courage to put my arm inside her kennel, she took hold of it gently and held it. She didn't squeeze it. She didn't shake me. She didn't growl. She just held it. She looked right into my eyes and her whole body was shaking as though every inch of her was wagging. At that moment, I knew for sure that I loved dogs.

Annie weighed about sixty-five pounds, and I felt very small looking into her big, dark, intense eyes as she held my arm in her mouth. From that day onwards, every single time I walked by the kennel, I placed my arm in the kennel. She held it for a couple of minutes, and then I petted her and walked away.

All the Labradors seemed very fierce while they were out in the fields, but they were very sweet and docile when they weren't working. They went through years of training to reach a point where they could go off-leash in a field and retrieve birds, then bring them back and sit politely until they were told to go retrieve another one.

At a very young age, those Jack Russells and Labradors provided me with a perfect example of the difference between reactive and proactive dog training.

For a while after this, I wanted to become a vet. Over time, however, I became friendly with Jim, the trainer, and increasingly fascinated by the training process. My family was living in France at the time, and every time we came home for the holidays I watched Jim training the dogs. I wanted to be a part of it. Jim was a very calm, patient, and assertive man. Although he never dominated the dogs, he was always in total control.

My grandfather's property was huge, around 160 acres, and part of the dogs' daily regimen involved following Jim around in a golf cart that he drove all around the property. It was their exercise routine. That taught me the importance of providing dogs with physical stimulation.

I also watched Jim train the dogs to retrieve birds. He had a contraption that looked like a potato gun and shot a pillow-like toy about the size of a pineapple. At certain points along the trail he'd fire the gun, and one of the dogs would chase after the toy, bring it back, and sit or lay down and wait while the next dog took a turn.

I started to realize how capable dogs are of learning almost anything. One dog, which went by the name of Darby, left a particularly strong impression. Darby was blind. Jim adapted his routine by shooting the toy a little closer to the ground, so the noise made by the gun was more audible, and Darby was able to retrieve the toy guided only by his ears and his nose.

Darby wasn't born blind. He suffered from a congenital condition and as an adult dog gradually lost his sight over the course of about a year. His training was so strong, his drive to find the toy so powerful, that he could compensate using his sense of smell and his hearing. That was another key moment in realizing the power of conditioning.

AN INTENSE APPRENTICESHIP

After graduating from Berklee College of Music, I decided

to pursue my passion for working with dogs. I did some research on the internet and found a job opening at a company called Canine Protection International, or CPI.

CPI specialized in dogs that were trained to protect people, dogs such as German shepherds, Belgian Malinois, and Rottweilers. At the time, I was happy to get experience hanging out with dogs, so I applied to be a kennel tech. My job mainly involved feeding the dogs and cleaning out the kennels.

One day, one of the trainers was away, and the others offered me the chance to go upstairs to the training room and help them train. Naturally, I was pretty excited. I thought it was a great chance to get my foot in the door and start doing some training.

They were working mainly with German shepherds and Belgian Malinois, both big dogs, and I assumed we'd be training one of those. They told me they needed somebody to decoy the dog, which means someone who's going to play the role of the bad guy and take bites.

I went upstairs to the training room, and they gave me a flimsy sleeve called an undercover sleeve, to be worn under a hoody or jacket for a little bit of protection. Then they went downstairs and told me that when they came back up with a dog, I should present my arm out in front of me for a bite. I agreed, still anticipating that they'd come up with a sixty-five-pound Belgian Malinois.

When they returned, they had a 140-pound Rottweiler. The dog's name was Bodo, and he belonged to the actor Steven Seagal. He had a full grille of titanium teeth. The reason for the teeth was that he'd been kicked in the face by a horse and needed to have them replaced. I was like a deer in the headlights. I could only trust that the trainers had some level of control over this dog, because he was showing full aggression and coming closer and closer to me.

As the trainers brought Bodo within range, the dog grabbed my arm and shook. Rottweilers, when they bite, tend to hold on and shake their prey extremely hard. I weighed about 130 pounds at the time, and I was almost knocked off my feet. Eventually, the trainers commanded the dog to release, and I ripped off the sleeve. It was already coming up with huge welts and bruises.

Looking back now, it's clear there was no lesson the dog was learning from that session. It was a chance for the trainers to have some fun and haze the new guy. Nonetheless, it didn't put me off, and I've been working with dogs ever since.

TRAINING APPROACH

Years later, in 2010, I founded my own dog-training service, Walky Walk, in Boston. I take a coach approach to training now. Through one-on-one and an in-home style of training, I turn dog owners into dog trainers. It's imperative for owners to learn how to train their dogs. It is one of the most effective ways of building and enriching your relationship with your dog. "If I train my dog, will she still like me?" is a question I get quite often. Believe me when I tell you that by training your dog, you will greatly enhance your bond.

Since training is progressive, I help owners systematically by bringing a specific lesson plan designed for their specific goals. In order to reach that goal, owners must complete training lesson by lesson. We usually meet for one hour a week, which is not long enough for me to train the dog effectively, but it is enough time to train the owners. I can't be there for the rest of the week, so I rely on people making use of the suggestions I give them.

Once the owner has met the milestones for that session, he or she is ready to move on to the next phase of training. I come over again, bringing new material, and teach the next set of skills and exercises needed to reach the goals. As long as the owner is putting in the time and effort, training will be successful.

Jim once told me, "Dogs are a reflection of you. If they're doing something incorrectly, it's because you didn't teach them effectively." Dog training isn't rocket science. It doesn't have to be complicated. We don't need to reinvent dog training when we get a new puppy or have a behavior we need to work on. Be consistent and patient, and follow your plan. Remember, well-behaved dogs aren't born, they're trained.

YOU'RE ALREADY TRAINING YOUR DOG

The purpose of this book is to give you the tools you need to raise a happy and obedient dog, one that will be a delight to you and your family for years to come. You may wonder whether you really need to train your puppy, and the answer to that question is: you already are.

Dogs learn through repetition. If you bring home a puppy, and you don't train her proactively, your dog won't have any instructions as to what she should be doing. She will fill that void by doing whatever she wants. Even if you don't encourage your dog to jump up on you, or bark at the door, or beg at table, she may pick up those behaviors.

Here's a common example. When you get home, you're happy to see your dog. You get very excited, and the dog reciprocates. She jumps up on you. She starts to bark and whine. If you do that for a few months when you first get a puppy, you're teaching your dog that it's okay for her to enter a hyper-reactive, anxious state of mind when you walk through the door. The same is true when you leave. If you give your dog a grand, theatrical farewell, you can accidentally condition her to develop separation anxiety. Although you're not setting out to teach your dog to be anxious when you come home or leave the house, you're indirectly encouraging the behavior.

One of the most common problems I work on is adult dogs that get overexcited when their owner comes home. That's because the behavior took root when they were puppies. People think that they can encourage their dogs to jump up when they're small, and then easily change that behavior when the dog's grown. Unfortunately, it doesn't work like that.

The good news is that you only need to do a little training from day one to make sure that you're encouraging the behaviors you actually want your dog to display, and discouraging the ones you don't. Of course, if you like your dog jumping up on you, that's a different story. The golden rule is that if you're happy with how your dog's behaving, your dog is trained. If you want your dog to sleep in bed with you and you're comfortable with your dog begging for food, your dog's trained.

If you *don't* want your dog to do those things, however, it's important that you train your dog accordingly. Before you get a dog, it's an excellent idea to sit down for an hour or two and consider your expectations. Do you want your dog to sleep in a kennel, or do you want her to sleep in a bed? Do you want her to be allowed up on the furniture? Do you want her to eat in a specific area? Will she be allowed to beg at table? How do you want her to greet guests?

It's quite easy to train a puppy with specific goals in mind, and much more difficult to retrain an adult dog that has already formed strong habits. Time spent planning how you train your dog is time well spent. Imagine acquiring a German shepherd in the fall, only to discover in the spring that your six-month-old dog sheds her hair. If you've allowed your dog to lie on the couch, you'll soon find that your couch is covered in dog hair.

Sit down with anyone else who has a vested interest in how your dog behaves and think about the rules you want to put in place. With a little foresight, you can come up with a training plan that will guide your choices and help you raise a happy, healthy dog that will be a much-loved part of the family for years to come.

WHAT DOES A TRAINED DOG LOOK LIKE?

Dogs learn through conditioning. Training your dog is essentially conditioning her responses so that she behaves the way you want her to. Have you ever shaken a bag of dog treats and had your dog run towards you because she knows she's going to get a treat? That's conditioning in action. If you always jingle the leash when you're preparing to take your dog for a walk, your dog learns to come running whenever you jingle the leash.

To strengthen the power of your training and create lasting results, you need to tap into the power of conditioning.

Here's an example of how conditioning works, using my Belgian shepherd, Twitch.

Every single time I start preparing her meal, I put a scoop of food into her bowl. The food makes a jingling sound, which alerts Twitch to the fact that she's about to eat. She goes to her bed. I fill the bowl up with food, and then I go over to the sink, where I wet the food and set it down on the counter while it soaks. All this time, Twitch stays in her bed. Then I pour out the water, tell her to go to her crate, and she goes sprinting towards her crate.

Twitch does all this because right from the beginning I conditioned her responses. Whenever I prepared her food I would put her in her bed. After weeks of this she started going straight to her bed whenever she heard the food jingling in the bowl. Once I'd finished preparing the food, I told her to go to her crate, and she went running to the crate.

That's a very strong conditioned response. Every single time she hears the food hit the bottom of the bowl, she understands that if she goes to her bed, she will soon get to go to her crate and, after that, she will get to eat. This approach only takes about forty-five seconds for breakfast and forty-five seconds for dinner, so a total of perhaps ninety seconds of training per day. The key is consistency. Twitch's response comes from enacting the same routine every single day for months on end. She is over a year old now, and I'm still reinforcing the behavior.

The more training you do with your dog when she's very young, the less training you have to do when she's older. Before long, you will get to a point where your dog does things automatically, without even being told. You won't even need to tell her to go to her bed or her crate. She'll already be doing it.

That's proactive training. The alternative is reactive training. When you train reactively, you wait to see what your dog does, and then you scramble to eliminate the behaviors you don't want. It's a lot harder, and it's a lot more stressful, both for you and for your dog.

You can take your dog to a kennel and have her trained within two or three weeks, which is an incredibly short amount of time for a dog to learn everything you want her to learn. The downside to this approach is that a lot of corners will be cut. Your dog will be forced to do things she's not conditioned to do. Reinforcing a conditioned response is much different then forcing a new behavior.

I work a lot with people who have reached that stage. Typically, a client will tell me that the dog is reacting to other dogs or has tried to bite the client's kid's friend. It's still very possible to recondition and rehabilitate the dog, but it's so much more effective to get it right the first time.

DOGS ARE DOGS, PEOPLE ARE PEOPLE

One of the biggest obstacles to training dogs effectively is created by owners who try to humanize their dogs. As a result, they're reluctant to crate their dogs, to restrict them from running freely around the house, or to prevent the dog from being on the couch or the bed. At the extreme, I've seen people in downtown Boston dressing their dogs in sweaters and sunglasses, and pushing them around in strollers.

There's nothing malicious about humanizing dogs, and we all do it to some extent. When you're training a dog, however, it's important to resist the temptation as much as possible. Dogs don't learn like humans, and when you treat your dog like a human, you'll confuse her and send the message that she's more in control than she really is.

Then, when you want your dog to do something specific—for example, to get off the couch—you'll find it very difficult to exert control. This is true even if you want your dog to be primarily your companion. Train your dog well for the first year or two of her life, and then you can relax the rules while remaining in control. You can invite your dog onto the couch and let her loose in the house, without fearing that she'll be impossible to shift or that she'll start ripping up everything in sight. Attempt to reverse engineer that situation, however, and you'll run into trouble.

Some people resist crate training because they humanize their dogs and don't want to cause them any pain. They fail to train their dogs while they are still puppies, and then they find themselves with an adult dog that drives them mad by doing things they don't want them to do and won't stay calm in a crate. Reconditioning the dog at that point is a far more painful process than crate training a puppy, and requires a lot of corrections. If you love your dog and don't want to cause her pain, train her properly when she's young.

THREE PRINCIPLES OF SUCCESSFUL DOG TRAINING

In this book, we will cover three important components to training a happy and obedient dog: **socialization**, **housebreaking**, and **motivation**. Only after your dog's **motivation** and drives are at their highest possible levels will you move on to more advanced and formal obedience training. At first, keep it simple.

Socialization is the single most important aspect of training. Socialize your dog as a puppy by exposing her to her environment and introducing her to all walks of life. In this way, you'll have a well-rounded dog that feels confident and enjoys being around all kinds of people, is comfortable and happy going to new places, and likes the experience of being out and about.

I don't care if your dog can sit, lie down, go to the crate on command, and get you a beer from the fridge. If your dog is unfriendly and aggressive towards people and/or other dogs, it turns dog ownership into a liability. Make training your dog to be sociable your number-one priority.

Your second priority is **housebreaking**. Again, I don't care if your dog knows how to do a back flip. If she's going to the bathroom upstairs in your room every single night, what's that worth?

Your third priority, which you can begin working on simultaneously with socialization and housebreaking, is **motivation**. Motivation is the key to teaching and correcting wanted and unwanted behaviors. It's through the power of motivation that we'll teach our dogs basic and advanced behaviors. People will often ask me, "Tom, what's the hardest kind of dog to train?" My response is, "An unmotivated one."

Obedience training through motivation may not require utilizing complex commands such as walking without a leash or being able to recall your dog from fifty yards away in highly stimulating environments. It's more about maintaining some level of control over your dog. That will help to eliminate numerous unwelcome behaviors, and owning a dog becomes much more enjoyable when your dog is well behaved and under control. As discussed above, obedience training starts by developing your dog's motivation before using it to train her.

Motivation needs to be balanced and can be broken down into positive reinforcement and negative reinforcement. Positive reinforcement is adding something to make the outcome of a behavior or command more likely to happen. This can be rewards or corrections. Negative reinforcement is the removal of something to make a behavior or command more likely to happen. Here are a few examples of how to motivate your dog.

Every dog instinctually needs food to survive, so you can use that to your advantage in your training. Dogs work for food. Also, the nice thing about food is that it's very simple to manipulate a dog into different positions and behaviors. You can lure a dog on or off her bed. You can hold food right above her head and lure her into a sit. You can lure her downward and teach her how to lie down. Her motivation for food drives her to learn just about anything. I've had tremendous success with boiled chicken.

Another excellent way to motivate your dog is by using toys. All dogs have a natural instinct to catch things that move. If you have a tennis ball, for example, it stimulates them in a similar fashion as a small animal running away from them would. I prefer tug toys or a ball on a rope to incorporate toys for training.

Being social creatures, dogs thrive on being a part of something. I like to think praise has an element of camaraderie. You're involved in the training process as much as your dog is, and when you use praise correctly, it conveys appreciation, acceptance, approval, and enthusiasm for what she's doing or what she's done. Even though all dogs love to be praised, I find it even more effective when it's paired with either food or toys. It intensifies the reward and makes the experience of doing something correctly even more fun and desirable. Praise also helps you, the owner, become synonymous with the reward. Praise has to be believable and stimulate your dog, otherwise it's not effective.

Motivation through negative reinforcement is one of the most misunderstood aspects of dog training. Often confused with "positive punishment," negative reinforcement is simply the removal of something to make the outcome of a command or behavior more likely to be repeated on a more reliable basis. Depending upon your goals for your dog, you may not use this concept at all. Negative reinforcement is solely used to enhance and proof train once a dog already has a very solid foundation in the behaviors you wish to advance, and you should *never* attempt to use this approach to teach your dog a new behavior. Many people buy a prong collar or an electric collar and think that as soon as they pop or shock their dog, their dog will do what they want, like a remote would a TV. It doesn't work like that. In fact, this is a horrible way to train a dog. Prong collars and electric collars are only effective when the dog understands the concept of negative reinforcement. Your dog needs to feel in control during this phase, which is why you should only layer it on top of behaviors the dog already knows extremely well.

THE CHOICE IS YOURS

To reiterate, there's no such thing as not training your

dog. Whatever you do, you're conditioning your dog's behavior from the moment you bring her home. Take the time to plan ahead and train your dog while she's still a puppy, and you can set yourself up for years of joy. Make the mistake of thinking you can easily reverse unwanted behaviors when your dog's two or three years old, and you're asking for a lot of totally avoidable stress.

Over the following chapters, you'll learn everything you need to know to set your home up for a new puppy, along with training techniques that will prepare you to train your pup proactively. Take them to heart, and you'll set yourself on the road to having a dog that is fully potty trained, calm both in and out of the crate, sociable, and obedient—a dog that is a delight to you and to anyone else your dog comes into contact with.

Ignore the steps laid out here, and you may still get lucky. You may have a particularly good-natured dog. You may live in an area where obedience training isn't a necessity. You may have a high tolerance for challenging behaviors. Alternatively, you may find that, when your dog is a year old, you can't get her off the couch, she barks all night, and she reacts poorly around other dogs. Take control of that process, and you won't just have to hope for the best.

CHAPTER 1

Preparing Yourself and Your Home for a Puppy

CHOOSING A BREED

Everyone gets a dog for a different reason, so it's important that you understand why you want a dog, and why you're choosing the breed that you're choosing. Some people want a dog purely for companionship. Others want a working dog, a lapdog, or even a show dog. There are hundreds of different breeds of dogs, and each one is bred for a specific reason. If you're not clear from the start why you're getting a dog, it can lead to complications further down the line.

Start by knowing what you're going to do with your dog. Perhaps you want a buddy. Perhaps you want to teach your kids some responsibility. Perhaps you had a dog when you were growing up and want to relive that experience.

Alternatively, perhaps you live in a bad neighborhood and you want a working dog for protection. Perhaps you're blind or partially sighted, and you need a guide dog. What will your relationship be like? What behaviors will you want from the dog when she's older?

Many people choose a dog based purely on what they look like, even if the breed isn't suitable for their lifestyle. Don't fall in love with a particular breed. Do some research into different breeds and choose based on the characteristics you want your dog to exhibit.

Ultimately, you'll love whatever dog you choose. Even people who own Chinese crested dogs, which are consistently voted the ugliest dogs in the world, grow to love them. Nonetheless, some dogs will be much more suitable than others for your lifestyle. If you choose a border collie purely because you had one when you were growing up, or because you've seen one on TV and you loved her, you may not be able to meet that dog's needs.

At the time of writing, I'm working with a client who owns two Australian shepherds and lives in a small apartment in Cambridge, Massachusetts. Australian shepherds are sheep herding dogs. They're bred to work in huge fields and herd cattle. They come from long lines of herding and sporting champions, and they're highly driven. They are poorly suited to live in a small apartment in Cambridge.

Even though they're getting a long walk every day, those dogs bark a lot and exhibit symptoms of anxiety. The owner chose them because he heard how intelligent they are, but is now dealing with a lifetime of powerful, challenging behaviors. Training an intelligent dog isn't necessarily easier. They would be perfectly suited for an experienced and active dog owner who likes to take them running and plans on doing some type of dog sport, such as agility. That same experienced and active person would probably regret choosing an English bulldog, which is a breed with low energy levels and lower stamina.

Instead of choosing a dog because you like the look of the breed, think about what you want from the dog and choose a breed that suits you. Consider investing in a copy of D. Caroline Coile's *The Dog Breed Bible*, which describes all breeds, details their temperaments, and explains what they were originally bred for. It also gives you information about the types of foods that are good for them, whether they're good with children, and much more.

If my client had looked at that book before he decided which breed of dog to get, he would have seen that Australian shepherds require about four hours of exercise every day, and at least 3,000 square feet. Maybe he would have reconsidered.

TABLE 1.1: CHARACTERISTICS OF COMMON BREEDS

BREED	AREA OF ORIGIN	ORIGINAL FUNCTION	COAT AND COLOR	HEIGHT AND WEIGHT	TEMPERAMENT	UPKEEP
Labrador Retriever	Canada	Water retrieving	Short, straight, and fairly hard coat. Solid black, yellow, or chocolate.	Male: 22.5–24.5" tall/65–80 lbs. Female: 21.5–23.5" tall/55–70 lbs.	Devoted, obedient, and amiable, Labs are good with everyone. They are eager to please and enjoy learning, but they can be hardheaded. They love to swim and retrieve.	Labs need daily exercise, preferably retrieving and swimming, as well as mental exercise. The Lab coat needs weekly brushing to remove dead hair.
Australian Shepherd	USA	Sheepherding	Straight to wavy, medium-length coat. Blue merle, black, red merle, or red, all with or without white markings and/or tan points.	Male: 20–23" tall/50–65 lbs. Female: 18–21" tall/40–55 lbs.	Bold, alert, confident, independent, and responsive. Without mental/physical stimulation, they become unruly. Reserved with strangers. They often herd children and other small animals.	Aussies need a good, strenuous workout every day, combining both physical and mental challenges. The coat needs brushing or combing one to two times a week.
Boston Terriers	USA	Ratting, companion	Short, smooth coat. Brindle, seal, or black with markings on muzzle, between eyes, and forechest; possibly white collar and lower legs.	15–17" tall/10–25 lbs. (25 lbs. max)	Bostons are saucy, playful, devoted, and sensitive to their owner's moods. Somewhat stubborn, they nonetheless learn readily. Reserved with strangers, and may be aggressive toward strange dogs. Some bark a lot.	Love games, and most of their exercise needs can be met with a romp in the yard. Some Bostons wheeze and snore, and most don't tolerate heat well. The coat requires only occasional brushing.
English Bulldog	England	Bull baiting	Smooth, short coat. Brindle, solid white, red, or fawn, or any of these on a white background.	12–15" tall/Males weigh around 50 lbs. and females weigh around 40 lbs.	Jovial, comical, and amiable, among the most docile and mellow of dogs. They are willing to please, though they have a stubborn streak. They are generally good with other pets.	Short walks in cool weather. Overexertion, or exertion in hot, humid weather is dangerous. Bulldogs cannot swim. Most wheeze, snore, and drool. Tail folds and facial wrinkles should be cleaned daily.
Pug	China	Lapdog	Short, smooth coat.	10–11" tall/14–18 lbs.	Pugs are a blend of dignity and comedy. They are amiable, playful, and confident. They can be stubborn and headstrong but are generally willing to please.	Pugs need a short to moderate walk or a good play session daily. They do not tolerate heat. They need minimal coat care but daily cleaning of the facial wrinkles. They wheeze and snore.
French Bulldog	France	Lapdog	Short, smooth. Brindle, fawn, white, brindle and white.	11–13" tall/not to exceed 28 lbs.	Frenchies are clowns that enjoy playing as much as cuddling. They are amiable, sweet, companionable, and willing to please but somewhat stubborn.	Frenchies enjoy a romp or short walk but not in hot weather. They cannot swim. They snore and wheeze. The coat requires minimal care, but facial wrinkles should be regularly cleaned.
German Shepherd	Germany	Sheepherder, guardian, police dog	Straight, harsh, medium length. Black and tan, red and tan, all black, bicolor, and sable.	Male: 24–26" and 80–95 lbs. Females: 22–24" and 65–75 lbs.	Devoted, dependable, and biddable. They are aloof and suspicious toward strangers, protective of home and family. They can be domineering as well as aggressive toward other dogs.	Need a long walk or jog daily, along with challenging mental stimulation. The coat needs brushing one or two times a week.

CHOOSING A BREEDER

Choose a reputable breeder. Breeders who own their own business or have solid relationships with the owners have a greater investment in caring for their puppies and giving you good service. For insider information, talk to local vets and dog owners. If you're looking for a Labrador and see someone on the street or at the park who has one, ask where the dog was purchased, and whether or not the experience with the breeder was a good one.

Another option is online research. Look up local dog breeders and read reviews, and then visit them and talk to them in person. When you do, think of it as an interview. Good dog breeders will be as invested in making sure you can give the dog a good home as you are in making sure they care for their puppies.

Expect the breeder to interview you, too. If questions don't go any further than "Do you have a yard?" that's a red flag. A good breeder will vet you as a potential owner, and you should do the same to the breeder. Go beyond reviewing the dog's pedigree and ask as many questions as you can. You may want to know how many litters the mother has had, or whether she has any record of a particular health condition. What is the dog's father's temperament like? How would you rate the mother's energy level? Has the dog been exposed to kids? What was the dog like around the children? Which puppy do you think would be the best fit for X, Y, and Z situations? The more questions you ask, the more likely you will be to receive the best puppy for you.

Stay well away from puppy mills or businesses with the same ideology, because they don't take a lot of care over the quality or health of their dogs. Their dogs are often inbred, leading to a lot of health and behavioral issues. A good breeder won't breed a dog that suffers with a degenerative disease, but a puppy mill is little more than a huge warehouse of dog crates. There's very little control and very few breeding standards. Puppy mills only continue to operate because people buy from them, so do your research to find a great breeder so you can encourage better standards and professionals who genuinely care about their dogs.

Another type of breeder to avoid is the backyard breeder. These people are usually amateurs who mate their dogs with their neighbors' dogs in an effort to bring in some extra money. They don't usually know what they're doing, and when you buy from them, you're encouraging a lowering of breeding standards. German shepherds typically weigh between fifty and ninety pounds, have square hips, and are prone to hip dysplasia. A good breeder will be aware of the risks and won't breed any dogs that show signs of hip dysplasia. A backyard breeder probably won't notice or care.

In summary, buy your dog from someone who takes pride in what they do. Look for a place that's clean, with enough space for the dogs, and where you get the sense that both the breeder and the dogs themselves are friendly. Stay away from the extremes of industrialized puppy mills and amateurish backyard breeders, and ask plenty of questions to make sure that you understand and trust your breeder.

ADOPTING A RESCUE DOG OR PUPPY

I believe rescuing a dog is one of the most noble things someone can do. However, as well intentioned as one might be, the new owner may find herself with a handful, and a dog she didn't know she was adopting. If you're considering adopting a rescue dog or puppy, it's especially important to be clear about your motivations. Harsh as it may sound, rescue dogs are usually given away for a specific reason. If you don't know what that reason is, you may be in for a nasty shock. Some people adopt a rescue dog because they want an addition to the family, and discover six months later that the dog was given away because it acted aggressively towards small children. Suddenly, they've got a dangerous dog on their hands, and more than likely, the dog will be returned to the shelter again.

If you want to save a dog's life, perhaps because she's at risk of being euthanized, or you want to give a dog a better quality of life, then you're well-suited to adopting a rescue dog. In that case, your expectations for owning the dog are in line with your reasons for adopting her in the first place. You understand that the dog may need some additional training. You understand that you'll likely encounter some issues, and you're ready for that. Adopting a dog can be like a box of chocolates. You don't always know what you're going to get.

The Animal Rescue League is a good place to adopt dogs. The MSPCA (or other state SPCA) is another good place. Look for a place that you like, where you appreciate the set-up and what it stands for, and where you feel they do a good job placing dogs.

Just as you would when buying from a breeder, ask very specific questions. The most helpful thing you can know is why the dog was surrendered. How was she around the vet? Good around the other dogs? Shy? Is the dog confident? How was she around the staff? Be honest and say, "Here's why I'm adopting a dog. Which one is best for that reason?"

While I highly encourage rescuing dogs, owners need to be ready to accommodate a wide variety of temperaments and personalities, and give the dog what it needs.

ESSENTIAL EQUIPMENT

Once you've done your research and chosen your breed, or settled on a rescue dog that you're sure you can take care of, you'll need to prepare your home for the new arrival.

There are things your dog will need from the moment you bring her home. Chief among those are food, dog bowls, a crate, and a blanket. Your dog may come from the breeder with a travel crate, but she may not, so make sure you know what to expect, and prepare adequately. A harness can be a very useful tool for handling a small puppy. You can pick her up by the harness. You can give her a little tug to redirect her to a specific spot in the yard where you want her to go to the bathroom.

Before you bring the dog home, get a clear idea of where you want to locate the crate. Are you going to keep the crate in the bedroom? Are you going to keep it in the downstairs living room? Are you going to keep it in a spare bedroom? Are you going to keep it in the basement? All of these spots have potential advantages and disadvantages, so take a little time to determine what you think will work best.

Typically, the breeder will use a specific food, and it's a good idea to decide whether you want to continue using the same food or switch to a different brand. Occasionally, the breeder will supply a leash and collar, but in most cases, you'll need to make sure you have a leash and collar or harness ready.

A young dog will tug on her leash. She will probably bite the leash too, so that when you try to walk in one direction the dog can't easily be moved. For that reason, choose something fairly broad and robust. Nylon collars and harnesses are a better option than expensive leather ones at this stage, because they're cheaper and you're going to go through a few collars or harnesses over the course of the dog's life. If you invest in something expensive, you'll need to replace it in a few weeks or months.

When choosing a harness, you can usually determine which breeds each size is suitable for by looking at the package. At this point, your puppy's comfort is paramount. Although it's important to keep your goals in mind, stay calm and relaxed and don't think too far ahead. It's not realistic to expect a small puppy to walk on a loose leash or come on command. As long as you can get through the first few weeks of training, you're doing well. A harness will help you do that, and it's more comfortable for your dog than a collar.

If you're bringing home a very young puppy, your dog has only been alive for perhaps eight weeks. She's only had her eyes open for three to four weeks. Now she finds herself in a totally new environment, with almost no experience of how to handle that. Anything you can do to reduce stress levels will help, and trying to do too much too soon will only add to the stress. That's not an excuse to invite the dog up onto the bed or the couch. Those are surefire ways to humanize the dog and create issues later on. It's more about establishing an area for the crate; getting a good, healthy food; and creating a safe, controlled environment.

Give your puppy some chew toys to play with. Chew toys can definitely reduce stress and give the puppy a positive experience. A Nylabone is a good option. You should be able to find a Nylabone kit that covers the first three stages of a puppy's development in most pet stores. The first bone is for puppies aged eight to twelve weeks. The next one is for puppies that are teething. The third is for when they're six months and older. The key here is to stimulate your dog and give her something to do. Dogs can relieve a lot of stress on their own if they have something to chew on.

At this age, your dog's primary activities will be eating, sleeping, and answering the call of nature. Make sure you have a water bowl and poop bags or a poop scoop. Designate a bathroom area for your puppy outside.

A dog bed beside her crate will encourage your dog to

think of the bed as her safe space, and to feel comfortable there. Some dogs will adapt quickly to having their own beds. Others will try to play with it at first.

This phase, which is really about meeting the puppy's basic needs, will last for a week or two. Take your time and don't get ahead of yourself. Concentrate on making sure the dog is comfortable and at home in her new surroundings. Once that's achieved, you're ready to move on to the next step.

WHY SHOULD I CRATE MY PUPPY?

Crate training is the most powerful tool you have to prevent your dog from developing unwanted behaviors. If your dog is in a crate, she can't be chewing on the rug. If your dog is in a crate, she can't be urinating in the corner. If your dog is in a crate, she can't be destroying shoes.

Many people want to know when their dog should be in the crate. The simple rule to remember is that if you can't give your dog 100 percent of your attention, that dog needs to be in the crate. As I write this, my puppy Twitch is in her crate. She's over a year old now, and I'm still reinforcing the training.

There is one exception to this rule: if you have a small

room, such as a mud room, or a gated area in your house or apartment that has nothing your puppy is likely to chew on, you can use that instead of a crate. The principle is the same, however. Whenever you can't give your dog 100 percent of your attention, she needs to be in a controlled environment.

The big advantage of doing this is that it doesn't ever allow your dog to develop satisfaction from bad behaviors such as chewing on the furniture or peeing on the rug. Those things simply don't become part of her repertoire. Then, when you do reach a stage where you're ready to let your dog out of the crate, she won't be motivated to chew on socks or bark out the window. Those behaviors will have never taken root.

Getting your dog accustomed to her crate is a big part of training. If she can't be calm, quiet, and collected inside the crate, there's no way she's going to be calm, quiet, and collected outside the crate. Outside the crate is a much larger environment, with much more stimulation. If you try to get ahead of yourself and bypass the crate process, you're setting yourself up for an enormous amount of agony further down the road.

Crate training is also very useful for building your dog's food drive, which you will use to train her. Feed your dog in the crate. When you put food in the crate, and the only thing that's in the crate is food, she'll focus on it straight away. She has nothing else to do. The most stimulating thing in the crate is her food. Do this regularly, and you will start your dog on the right path to developing a regular mealtime and, most importantly, a healthy food drive.

Another advantage of crate training is that it provides a controlled environment to help you teach your dog where she can and can't go to the bathroom. Again, if you can't teach your dog not to go to the bathroom inside the crate, you've got a small chance of teaching her not to go to the bathroom elsewhere inside the house. It's simple repetition. Whenever you take your dog out of her crate, attach her to a leash, or to a harness and collar, and take her to the spot you've designated outside for her to go to the bathroom. If she doesn't go, take her back to the crate and try again ten or fifteen minutes later. If it helps the puppy to move quickly outside, don't hesitate to pick her up and briskly walk to her designated spot and put her down. Some puppies will attempt to relieve themselves on their way out.

Once your dog goes to the bathroom where you want her to go, you may leave her out of the crate for a while knowing she's just emptied her bladder. Give her a toy to play with. At this point, you're conditioning the dog to know that, once she uses the bathroom outside, she gets a little playtime with a Nylabone, with another dog if you have one, or with you.

In the wild, dogs and wolves will always seek out a place to sleep that offers quiet and security. You won't find a wolf sleeping in the middle of a field. A crate is the domestic equivalent of that. It has one way in, and one way out.

The idea of crate training often brings up a lot of resistance. People feel that it's cruel. They may get home from work, play with the puppy for a while, and then, when they go to bed, be reluctant to put the puppy back in her crate. The reality is that dogs should spend more time in their crates then you might think. There's a time for dogs to experience more freedom, and being a puppy is not one of those times. The more control over their experiences, the better off they'll be later.

While crate training is an indispensable tool for training your dog, it's important that you don't neglect other elements of training. Make sure that you take your dog out to parks and on field trips, and begin to socialize her. Always remember, however, that if you can't give your dog 100 percent of your focus, she needs to be in her crate. If you go to the grocery store, crate your dog. If you go upstairs to work, crate your dog. When you're sleeping, crate your dog.

Many people find this very difficult to accept, and it's one of the most prevalent ways in which owners humanize their dogs. They hear whining, and they think the dog wants to come out of the crate. That may be true in the short-term, but in the long-term it really is in the dog's best interests to be crate trained.

Dogs do occasionally have accidents in the crate, particularly when they're very young and they haven't developed the bladder and sphincter control they need to hold it. It's a good idea to take your dog out to go to the bathroom every couple of hours at first. If you leave her in the crate too long, she'll lose control of her bladder or bowels and will have to relieve herself.

It's also important to recognize that this isn't an exact science, even for a dog trainer. When I brought Twitch home, I was determined that she would *never* have an accident in the crate. Ten minutes later, she'd pooped in the crate. With time and consistency, however, she got the idea, and now she's perfect.

Ultimately, you're crate training your dog not to restrict her freedom, but to feel comfortable giving her *more* freedom when she's older. My older nine-year-old pit bull, Ripley, has complete run of the house now. That's because he was crated for the first two years of his life. I can go out for ten hours, and when I return, I find him in almost the exact same spot I left him. No barking. No chewing. No climbing on the furniture. Crate training isn't evil. It's simply a necessary process of conditioning and training a well-behaved dog.

There's much, much more stimulation outside a crate than inside, so a puppy that can't behave herself inside a crate has no prospect of doing so outside. If your puppy's stimulated by hearing a sound while she's in her crate, she'll be ten times more stimulated by the same sound while she's in the living room, or by seeing someone walk around outside the window.

Some people are tempted to abandon crate training because the dog whines while inside the crate and stops when let out. What they're doing, however, is conditioning the dog to understand that if she whines she'll be let out of the crate. Next time, the dog whines louder and longer. It can be a little hard to hear your dog whine when she's in the crate, but the benefits later on far outweigh the inconveniences now.

Be prepared, however, to adapt your plans if they aren't working. You may find that your puppy whines a lot when the crate's in the bedroom, and moving her downstairs alleviates the problem, or vice versa.

A blanket draped over your dog's crate will help minimize stimulation. If your dog is crated in the living room, she may be stimulated by seeing people, or by the TV, or by another dog or a cat. Using a blanket will help eliminate the visual stimulation, which can help your dog to settle.

By the time your dog is a year and a half or two years old, you should be able to leave the door of the crate open for your dog to come and go as she pleases. She will sleep in there or go inside when she needs a rest, and she will be free to wander around the house, but you won't have to worry about her chewing things, barking at people, or going to the bathroom inside the house. She will be calm in the crate, calm in the house, and calm when you take her outside. Those are hallmarks of a dog that has been properly crate trained.

HOW DO I CHOOSE A CRATE?

The first thing to be aware of is how big your dog will become as an adult. If you have a small dog that's only going to reach fifteen pounds, you'll want a very different crate than if you have a very big dog that'll grow to 200 pounds. Most crates you'll find come with clear indications of their dimensions and a list of breeds that they're suitable for.

There are two primary varieties of crate. The first is called a Vari Kennel or travel crate, and the second is a traditional wire crate. A Vari Kennel has a plastic base, a plastic top, and grating on the side, with a swing door. They're quite enclosed, so they do a good job of mimicking the experience of a den. Wire crates are more open, although you can easily throw a blanket over them to recreate the effect.

Wire crates work well because they usually come with dividers and, ironically, travel just as well as Vari Kennels. They're also very easy to assemble and fold up. You should be able to find a wire crate that will be suitable for your dog throughout her life. When she's very young, give her just enough space to stand and turn around. Then, as she grows, gradually move the divider back.

The reason for restricting the amount of space your dog has is that dogs rarely go to the bathroom in an area that they have to sleep in. If they have a lot of space in the crate, they may be able to eliminate at one end and sleep at the other, which will make house training more difficult.

Too much space within the crate can also contribute to neurotic behavior. A dog in an excessively large crate may become anxious and start to walk in circles. If your dog has too much room to move, or if she can do laps inside the crate, the crate's too big.

A Vari Kennel won't be suitable throughout your dog's life. You'll need at least two or three. You will probably need one for use between eight and sixteen weeks, another from sixteen weeks to six months, and a third from six months to two years and beyond. Nonetheless, it's a good idea to have more than one crate.

It's not a good idea to allow your dog to travel loose in the car, for exactly the same reason that crate training is essential. If you don't have a crate in the car, you run the risk that your dog will bark out the window, pee on the seat, or become carsick from running back and forth across the seat. She may even jump into your lap while you're trying to drive. To save time assembling and disassembling a single crate, keep a second one in the car.

Another reason to have additional crates is if you have a family member who looks after the dog on a regular basis. If you visit mom and dad or grandma and grandpa every couple of weeks, it's much more convenient for them to have their own crate.

It can be useful to take your dog's crate with you on field trips so that she has somewhere to get away to if she becomes stressed or tired. Keep the crate in the car and, if necessary, turn the air conditioning or heat on to keep her cool or warm enough. Alternatively, you can find a nice quiet spot for your dog to relax when she needs a break, and keep the crate there.

If you have a relatively small car, keep an extra crate in the trunk so you can access it easily, assemble it quickly, and be ready to go. If you have a large car, you may have room to keep additional assembled crates in there permanently. However many crates you choose to buy, and however you choose to organize them, focus on making them as convenient as possible to use. Over the long-term, that will make it much more likely that you stick to your plans.

If there is zero chance of assembling a crate in your car because it's simply too small, figure out a way to secure your dog to a specific seat as you drive. They have special harness attachments so that you may keep your dog in one area in the vehicle. Limit your dog's freedom in the car in some capacity.

SELECTING A FOOD

Choose a quality food for your puppy. It may be tempting to try to save money on a cheap food, but it's a false economy. Premium food will boost your dog's food drive and has numerous other positive effects.

Try to stay away from any food that contains wheat, corn,

or soy. Those ingredients are cheap filler proteins, and dog food producers use them to bulk up low quality foods in an effort to make more money. They may be easy and convenient, but they will impact negatively on your dog's health. Take the time to go to a quality pet store and source a high quality brand. Pawsh Dog Boutique on Newbury and Gloucester Streets is my go-to in Boston.

Pound for pound, premium foods cost more than cheap foods. Nonetheless, they're actually better value. They contain denser, higher quality proteins, such as salmon and chicken, and real fruits and vegetables that contain the vitamins and minerals your dog needs to thrive. You can feed your dog much less of a premium dog food and still meet her nutritional needs, so you may end up paying less per meal than you would pay for low quality food. As a rough comparison, you may need five cups of a low quality food per day, whereas one and a half to two cups of a premium food may be enough.

Naturally, if you're putting five cups in, five cups will come out. A healthy dog should be eliminating as many times per day as she eats. If your dog eats three meals per day, she should have three bowel movements. Feed her low quality dog food, however, and she may need to defecate five, six, or even seven times per day. That will make potty training a lot more stressful and will have an impact on your dog's health. It's a lot of work for your dog's digestive system to be digesting that much food, and it will take its toll. A premium food will end up saving you money on trips to the vet, so be sure to factor that in when you make your choice.

I saw a client recently who asked me whether it was normal for her dog to be eliminating seven times a day, with very soft bowel movements, even though she was only feeding the dog twice a day. We switched her dog to a premium food, and within a couple weeks, her dog was eating much less and eliminating much less, with much healthier movements.

Do your research and choose a food that will give your puppy the nutrients she needs to thrive. An excellent independent resource to determine which food will suit your dog best, and also warn you about brands of food that are poor quality and will be detrimental to your dog, is www.dogfoodadvisor.com. A good pet shop should be able to advise you as well. Don't worry about giving your dog the most amazing food available, but make sure you're avoiding the cheap ones.

A similar principle applies when deciding what food to use for treat training.

Milk bones and dog biscuits can taste bland and take

dogs a long time to eat, so they make poor foods for treat training. Your dog needs to be over the moon for the food you're using for training. Chopped up chicken is instantly exciting to a dog. I've worked with clients who thought their dogs had low food drives, and as soon as I've shown the very same dogs some chicken, their entire demeanors have shifted. They've gone from being uninterested in treat training to becoming extremely engaged and excited, all because of the quality of the reward available to them.

You can also try hot dogs, or cheese, or even steak if you're prepared to pay the extra. Cheese and hot dogs can sometimes cause loose stools, so use them sparingly until you're sure they don't upset your dog's stomach. Chicken doesn't have that effect, even in quite high quantities, which is why it's such a good choice.

You can prepare chicken for training however you want. Fry it in oil, bake it, or grill it. The method I use is to boil a chicken breast in water for half an hour to forty-five minutes, until it's cooked through. After that, put it in the fridge for a while to harden and make it easier to chop. That saves it from coming apart into shreds as you chop it, which doesn't affect its value to the dog, but does make it harder to handle. Once it's hard enough, chop it into small pieces and keep it in a Ziploc bag.

CHOOSING A VET

Before you bring your puppy home for the first time, make sure that you have a vet lined up for the first series of shots. Most puppies will have had some shots before eight weeks old, but they'll need others by the time they reach sixteen to twenty weeks.

Choosing a vet for your puppy is one of the most important decisions you'll make, so take it seriously. Search online and read the websites of some local vets, and look up some reviews. If you find places that have negative reviews, find out why and consider moving on. Think about how easy it will be for you to travel to your vet at least twice a year, possibly in an emergency, and choose one within easy reach.

Seek out word of mouth recommendations, particularly those that focus on a specific practitioner, as opposed to an entire practice. A visit to the vet is potentially a very stressful experience for your dog, so do what it takes to find a vet who treats your puppy with kindness and competence, and who genuinely likes dogs. If you get a referral, mention it to the vet when you have your first appointment. It'll help to develop a bond between you and the vet, which can only increase the quality of care your dog receives.

Look for small, crucial gestures that indicate whether a vet likes her job. Does she take the time to make your puppy feel comfortable and to explain what's happening? Does she talk quietly and slowly, in a calming voice? Does she come down to the dog's level and allow the dog to approach her? Does she ask questions about what the dog likes and offer to give your dog a treat? All of those are really positive signs.

Ask your vet whether she's comfortable with you bringing your dog in even when you don't have an appointment. If she is, take your dog for field trips to the vet, purely to socialize your dog with the staff, or get weighed, or play with the tug toy. This is a powerful technique because, however positive and friendly the staff, going for shots is always a slightly unpleasant experience. Take your puppy in when you don't have an appointment and do some treat training, and you'll condition her to see trips to the vet as largely positive experiences, with food, play, social interactions, and the occasional shot.

By contrast, if you turn up for an appointment and the vet seems rushed and is short with you, stay away. If she doesn't have time for you and your dog, or she's running late, she won't do the things that make a puppy feel comfortable. Any vet can give your dog shots and take an x-ray, but the experience can either be a stressful and confusing one for a small puppy or a reassuring and relaxed one. Choose a vet that cares enough to offer the latter.

The first time I took Twitch to my current vet, one of the administration staff saw that her ears were back and noticed instantly that she was a little shy. She came out from behind the counter, knelt down to Twitch's level, and asked me whether she could give her a treat.

When the vet tech prepared her to see the vet, the vet tech made sure that she sat at a slight angle, with her legs bent away from her, so they weren't squared up. She didn't look Twitch directly in the eye, which might have been interpreted as threatening, and she allowed Twitch to come to her. The vet took the time to get to know Twitch, and was kind and well-mannered. That's the level of service you should expect from your vet.

Contrast that with a previous experience. Twitch had some sort of gastrointestinal infection, and she was suffering with diarrhea and blood in her stool. I took her to see the emergency vet, and she took Twitch in the back to administer an IV.

As I sat waiting for her, I heard an eruption of barking, whining, and screaming. Shortly afterwards, the vet came out, handed me Twitch, and said: "You need to discipline your dog." She didn't have the time to make Twitch feel comfortable, or ask for my help, so she held her down and forced the IV into her. Twitch was pinned on her back, and her survival drives were triggered. As far as she was aware, she was fighting for her life. It was a horrible experience, and I'll never return to that vet. If you take your dog to a vet that operates in that way, you run the risk that your dog will become phobic and resist trips to the vet with a passion. Find a vet that cares enough to take good care of your dog.

Your puppy will need several shots at the start of her life, some even before she starts interacting with other dogs. If you want a social puppy, you'll want to make sure you get all the recommended shots as soon as you can, so you can take field trips to parks and into the city and give your puppy opportunities to meet other dogs and people. If you start taking your puppy out before she's had her shots, you're putting her at risk, because puppies are very susceptible to diseases.

Your vet will have a list of shots that your puppy needs, and at what ages. Assuming you've chosen a good breeder, they'll take care of the distemper, measles, and CPIV shots that a puppy needs before eight weeks of age. Check with the breeder to make sure. The breeder should keep a full family history, including pedigree, birth date, and veterinary records. If you live locally and you trust the vet your breeder uses, you may want to retain the same vet. If not, your breeder should be able to transfer the records directly to the vet of your choice.

If, for any reason, your puppy hasn't had these initial shots before you take her home, it's imperative you make arrangements to get them as soon as possible.

Between ten and twelve weeks, your puppy will need a DHPP shot: that's a distemper booster, adenovirus, parainfluenza, and parvovirus. Between fourteen and sixteen weeks, she'll need a DHPP booster; and between twelve and twenty-four weeks, a rabies shot. Between twelve and sixteen months, she'll require DHPP and rabies boosters; and then DHPP boosters every one to two years and rabies boosters every one to three years.

Some people resist vaccinating their dogs, but it's important to remember that the diseases these shots protect dogs from are horrific; most are both deadly and incurable. If you have any questions, consult your vet.

You'll also want to enlist someone to take care of your pup in the event that you need to be out of town for a few days: a friend, a neighbor, a family member, a pet care professional. This is a much better strategy than scrambling to find someone on short notice if something comes up and you can't be around for your dog. Some people forget to plan, and then, when they need someone, they're short of time to do research and they settle for anyone they can find.

DON'T FAIL TO PLAN

Bringing a dog into your household is a big decision, and many people take it far too lightly. They don't understand what their puppy's needs will be, and they don't prepare effectively for the new arrival. As a result, they put themselves in a reactive position before they've even started to train the dog. Don't make owning a dog any harder than it already is. Choose a breed that suits your lifestyle, take the time to think about what equipment you will need before you start, and introduce your dog to a calm environment where you're in control from the beginning. A little homework before the dog arrives will save you a lot of stress and give you the comfort of knowing you're well prepared.

2

CHAPTER

Bringing Your
Puppy Home

FIRST IMPRESSIONS COUNT

Most puppies are adopted at around eight to ten weeks of age. That's the ideal time to take them. Before that, they're too dependent upon their mothers. Beyond sixteen weeks, they're more independent, and they won't imprint upon you as well, making them harder to train. Until they're eight weeks old, puppies benefit a lot from being around the other members of their litter. Their mothers nurse them, clean them, and marshal the pack.

Tiny puppies also learn a lot socially by being part of their original pack. They learn how to inhibit their bites by wrestling and sparring with other dogs in the litter. When one nips too enthusiastically, the others' yelps alert them to the fact that they're biting too hard. This is an important part of socialization, and attempting to make up for it later takes a lot of unnecessary time and effort.

By eight to ten weeks, depending upon the breed, they're ready to be a little more independent. They can break away from the pack without compromising their development, but they're still very malleable. They need someone to imprint upon. That's the perfect time for you as an owner and trainer to come in and fill that role. A good breeder will know the exact moment when their puppies need to be adopted and help you select a pup at the perfect time.

Once that window closes, beyond ten weeks, they become more and more strongly imprinted on the environment they're in. If they're still with their birth family at sixteen weeks, they'll grow up being more interested in other dogs than in humans. They may become dependent on the company of dogs and may experience anxiety without them. Weaning them from their mother at that time can cause separation anxiety and other insecurities, and they'll be harder to train.

Between eight and sixteen weeks is also a key time to boost your puppy's natural drives. Every dog has numerous natural drives, including food drive, toy drive, prey drive, and pack drive. Focus especially on building your dog's food drive and toy drive, and she'll be much more motivated to train.

If your puppy is a little older, you'll notice that she moves more quickly than an eight-week-old puppy, and is more easily stimulated. A puppy that's had a strong foundation between eight and sixteen weeks will be ready to learn more advanced behaviors, but don't think you can skip the foundations purely because your puppy is a little older.

First impressions are everything, so make your puppy's first few experiences in your home as positive as you possibly can. Anything you can do to take care of your dog's basic needs and make her feel comfortable will help. Give her some social interactions with you and anyone else in the home, but stay sensitive to your dog's temperament. Some puppies are confident; others are much more shy. If you have a big family, be considerate. Don't let five or six people compete to hold and pet the puppy all at the same time. Sometimes the best thing you can do for your puppy is to give her a break in the crate, where there's much less stimulation and she can relax and rest.

Expect the unexpected. Training your puppy isn't an exact science, and no matter how well prepared you are, it won't go 100 percent according to plan. While it's important to have clear goals, it's equally important to be able to roll with the punches and adapt. Be prepared for your expectations to evolve as your relationship with your puppy develops, and be prepared to come up with new plans if your original ones don't work.

Accidents will happen. Puppies are prone to use the bathroom in places you don't want them to. They're hard-wired to chew on things. You're only human, too, so you're bound to make mistakes and learn along the way. Do your best to stay calm and in control and to teach your puppy with patience and positivity, and ultimately she'll reward you. If your puppy has an accident, try to understand *why* it's happened, particularly if it's happening repeatedly, and make an adjustment.

If you work a nine-to-five job, find someone who can take your puppy out to go to the bathroom a couple of times a day while you're at work. Small puppies don't have the bladder control to last all day without going to the bathroom, so if you leave them in the crate all day while you're at work, you'll almost certainly come back to find that they've had an accident. Ask a family member, friend, neighbor, or dog care professional to come relieve your puppy if you're unable.

It's important to realize that there is no blueprint you can follow that's 100 percent guaranteed to give you a perfect puppy. It doesn't work like that. They're living creatures with minds of their own. The more confidence and security you can foster in your puppy, the easier she'll be to train and the more of her personality you'll see emerging.

A confident dog can go into any situation and be comfortable. If your dog's insecure, she'll become very cerebral and worried, and be constantly looking for an escape route. She won't feel safe, and she won't know what's coming next. Insecurity can breed fear, which can be extremely uncomfortable for the dog and, in some instances, can lead to a bite.

Proper training enhances your relationship with your dog, because it helps your dog become the truest version of herself. Twitch, my Belgian shepherd, is a very sensitive dog, and quite shy, so I do everything I can to make her feel as bold and confident as possible.

ESTABLISHING A FEEDING ROUTINE

Depending upon the size and breed of your dog, decide whether she needs to eat one, two, or three times per day, and stick to that. Most young puppies need three meals a day.

To complement the crate training you're already doing, feed your dog in her crate, and expect her to start eating it immediately. The crate will become synonymous with the food her body requires, making the crate a necessary part of her life. Also, feeding your dog in the crate and teaching her to eat the food quickly strengthens her relationship with food. Many people free-feed their dogs, meaning that they leave a bowl of food out all day long and allow their dogs to eat whenever they feel like it. That communicates to the dog that food is always available, and reduces its value, making training with food more difficult.

Some puppies are born with very high food drive. Others are born with much lower food drive. However strong your puppy's food drive, you can increase it by making food a limited commodity. Ultimately, your goal is to get your dog to the point where she eats her meals within two to three minutes. That's an indication that you've successfully increased your dog's food drive to a high level.

For a small puppy, it will take a while to reach that level of motivation. Initially, give her about five to ten minutes to eat her food, and gradually decrease the time over one to two months. If she hasn't started to eat within that five to ten minute timeframe, let her out of the crate and then take the food away and try again at the next meal. If she's still eating, however, let her finish. Five to ten minutes is a long time for a puppy to have food in front of her and not start to eat. If she hasn't started by then, it's time to take the food away. Do this consistently, and most puppies understand very quickly that they need to get it while the gettin's good!

To be absolutely certain, practice calling your pup out of her crate before you take her food bowl away, whether she's eaten it or not. Clap your hands, back up, and call her name so she comes to you. When she's out of the crate, take the food bowl and put it away. Use the opportunity to scoop her up and take her outside for a quick bathroom break. By the time you finish all that, any association between you and the removal of her food should be broken.

Never take the food away while the dog is actually eating. If you do that, you risk creating an association in the puppy's mind between you and the disappearance of her food, which she needs to live. That can lead to a behavior called "resource guarding" and, in some instances, a bite.

Here's a quick exercise to help reduce the chances of food guarding.

It starts with an empty bowl being placed inside the crate with your puppy already inside. Kneel down in front of the crate and place a second bowl filled with the puppy meal behind you. Wait for the puppy to investigate the bowl and realize there's nothing there. When she looks at you, place a handful of food in her bowl. As soon as she finishes the handful of food, wait until you get eye contact from the puppy. Again, place another handful of food inside the bowl. Repeat this until all the food is gone.

This exercise communicates with your dog that without you, her bowl is empty. She learns each time your hand comes near her bowl food appears. I recommend doing this a few times a week between eight and twenty-six weeks old.

If your puppy doesn't seem interested in her food, make sure that you're feeding her the right quantity and quality. Most foods have quite specific instructions on the back, and take into account the characteristics of different breeds. Working dogs need a lot more food than more sedentary breeds.

SOCIALIZING YOUR DOG

There is no more important part of training your dog than socialization. Dogs are social animals. They gain confidence from being a part of something. To encourage your dog to thrive, give her a place in the household, and spread the responsibility among everyone you want to have a relationship with the dog. First and foremost, you want to socialize the dog to you as the owner. If you don't have a good relationship with your dog, it's going to be a very long ride. The next priority is immediate family, especially any children in the household. After that, aim to introduce your dog to as many different kinds of people as possible. If you have children, consider giving each of them specific tasks. For example, assign one the job of giving the puppy breakfast, and another the job of giving the puppy an evening meal.

If you start to notice that the dog is favoring one person, make an effort to give her more positive experiences with other members of the household. It's common for a dog to establish very different relationships within the household, depending upon experiences and who takes care of her the most. To balance that tendency, make sure everyone takes a turn potty training, treat training, and toy training. Give everyone experience socializing the dog. It only takes a couple of minutes a day to build a relationship with the dog through play or treat training.

An effectively socialized dog will be comfortable inside and outside the home and adapt well to new situations. A poorly socialized dog may cause problems when you move to a new house or have children, or even when you take her to the park. Dogs draw very specific distinctions, so if you never introduce your dog to any black people, or white people, or men, or women, or people in uniform, or little old ladies, or people in big hats, that can cause problems when she does eventually encounter those categories of people. Make a checklist, and introduce your dog to as many different types of people as possible when she's small.

TABLE 2.1: SOCIALIZATION CHART

Use this chart as a guideline and for your own ideas on how to give your puppy exposure.

WEEKS YOU'VE HAD YOUR PUPPY/ DOG	ACTIVITIES/EXPOSURE					
Week 1	neighbor	puppy	extended family members	man sitting on a bench	causation eight-year-old girl	riding in the car
Week 2	woman with puffy coat	passerby near/outside home	a big dog	teenager on a skateboard	going to the vet	hanging out at the bus stop
Week 3	friends	small child (three to eight years old)	a Labrador retriever	older man with cane or walking stick	trip to pet store	ears being cleaned
Week 4	bathing your dog	elderly woman	a female miniature dog	person speaking in a different language	brushing your dog's teeth	barbecue
Week 5	nails being clipped/grinded	party	bully breed	a campfire	mother pushing stroller	riding an escalator
Week 6	little league game	inner city	woman wearing big hat and sunglasses	girl playing hopscotch	man with a beard	heavy machinery
Week 7	rural town	police officer	street vendor	African-American man	an old dog	someone on a bike
Week 8	riding the T or subway system	going to a soccer game	firefighter	girl hula-hooping	Asian woman	boy on a tricycle
Week 9	jogger	construction worker	camping	small group of children (two or more)	someone in a wheelchair	an open field
Week 10	5k race (not to run in but to socialize with crowd)	farm	lawnmower	river, pond, lake, or ocean	a very tall person	kids playing Frisbee™

The critical window for socialization is between eight and twenty weeks old. In that time, aim to introduce your dog to every type of individual you think she will meet over the course of her lifetime. You won't be able to cover every possible eventuality, but by introducing your dog to a broad range of people, you'll be preparing the way for her to be calm and relaxed when meeting new people later in life. Think about how people could appear different to a dog: a policeman or firefighter, for example, might trigger a dog that isn't used to seeing people in uniform. A child might trigger a dog that hasn't seen children before. A person on a bicycle might trigger a dog that has never seen a bicycle before.

Be sensitive to your dog's temperament. Ripley, my pit bull, is an exceptionally relaxed dog. I can take him to a big barbeque party, unleash him, and he simply goes up to people and watches them. He loves to be petted, and he's completely unfazed by all the people and the noise. Twitch, on the other hand, would find that environment extremely stressful. If your dog's shy, don't be tempted to throw her in the deep end by taking her somewhere with a lot of people and inviting those people to pet her. That strategy could backfire badly. Concentrate on the quality of socialization, rather than the quantity.

To do that, select the people you want to socialize your

dog with carefully. Let the dog approach the person, rather than vice versa. Ask people to take a treat from you to give your dog. That'll create a strong positive association in the dog's mind. Invite people you're socializing your dog with to play a brief game of tug with your dog.

Until you're certain that your dog is comfortable with people, prevent people from reaching in for your puppy. This is particularly true if your dog is already shy. Children, in particular, often lack the sensitivity to approach dogs slowly and carefully, which can contribute to your dog developing a phobia of children.

Another form of socialization is socializing your dog to different environments. Where do you envision yourself living over your dog's lifetime? If you live in a quiet neighborhood now but you're planning to move to the city, your dog could get a real shock when she's exposed to the hubbub of an urban environment.

To prevent that, take some field trips with your puppy. Even if you don't anticipate being in the city very much, a handful of trips while your dog's a puppy can make a big difference to her confidence. Begin familiarizing your dog with a range of environments by taking her to the grocery store or the pet store with you. Choose a place where you'll find a pet-friendly environment, but also enough stimulation to give your puppy new experiences. Even stores that don't welcome dogs will probably make an exception for a cute little eight-week-old puppy. As always, though, consider your puppy's temperament. If she seems happy and confident, keep going. If she seems shy and stressed, dial down the intensity a little by creating more distance from the stressor and shortening the experiences.

Socializing your dog is a great opportunity to test out her responses. Shy dogs do best when introduced to only one person at a time, in a low stimulation environment, until they become more confident. Bolder dogs may be comfortable in higher stimulation environments straight away. Always note any cues your dog's giving. If her tail's wagging and her tongue is out, she's clearly comfortable and relaxed. If her tail's between her legs or her hackles are up, get her out of that environment and try again, somewhere a little less stimulating, another day.

Be sure to bring some food with you when you socialize your dog. Receiving food from strangers is a great way for them to understand that people are friendly, and become more comfortable in social situations. Bring toys, too, to redirect them if they become a little stressed. Squeaky toys are particularly effective here. The sound captures their attention and activates their prey drive, which can quickly override whatever else they're experiencing.

Many of the most common reasons why people contact a dog trainer relates to dog reactivity and aggression, both of which have their roots in poor socialization, including over-socialization. Don't take a timid dog to a dog park, let her off the leash, and allow lots of other dogs to come and play with her. You might think you're acting in her best interests, but for a dog with a shy temperament, that's a very negative experience and can lead her to be uncomfortable around other dogs. As she grows older and bigger, she may become more dominant and even aggressive when confronted with other dogs.

To socialize a shy dog more effectively, find one other dog you can introduce her to. Choose slightly older dogs that won't move as quickly, and those of the opposite sex so that there's less chance of competition developing. Keep the interaction within a demarcated area, such as a yard with a fence, if possible. Give your dog a positive experience and an opportunity to become more confident, rather than a barrage of stimulation that will confuse and overwhelm her.

SHOULD I GO TO A DOG PARK?

Many people see dog parks as an opportunity to socialize their dogs, but they can do more harm than good. The vast majority of dogs in a dog park are unsupervised, running around off-leash with little to no feedback from their owners. It's important to keep your dog's socialization 100 percent positive, especially in the first few crucial weeks. Dog parks don't allow you to do that, because they don't allow you to stay in control of the experiences your puppy is having.

Almost every time I walk past a dog park, I see a scuffle break out. People justify that behavior on the basis that it's natural and the dogs are establishing a pecking order, but conflict can be very stressful for dogs, especially ones with a more reserved temperament, and especially when they're very young. An eight to sixteen week old puppy that finds herself regularly embroiled in fights is on the fast track to developing dog aggression or other undesirable behaviors. She's already learning that, in interactions with other dogs, she must either dominate or be dominated.

Another reason to be wary of dog parks is the high risk of disease from all the urine and feces your dog will come into contact with. When your puppy's very young, she may not even have had all her shots, so she could contract an illness from exposure to so many different bacteria and viruses.

Dog parks are at their worst during late afternoon and early evening, because people come home from work and want to take their dogs out for some exercise. During off peak hours, if you know all the other dogs in the park, they're a slightly different proposition. You have a bit more control, and you can take advantage of the enclosed area. I've worked with clients who live in the South End of Boston, and happen to be right across the street from Peter's Park, a dog park. They may find that the best option they have for exercising their dogs is to take them to the dog park at quiet times, when they trust the other dogs and owners. It's a far better option than going during rush hour with the unfamiliarity of who's there.

If you're planning to take your dog to a dog park, consult your vet beforehand, so you can be sure that your dog's had all the shots she needs to be safe. Whenever possible, however, choose a space that you have control over, with people you trust and dogs you know.

GROOMING

Different dogs require different grooming approaches. Some have short hair, and others have hair that grows long and needs to be clipped. Others shed their hair. When you're choosing your puppy, consider grooming requirements and make sure you're prepared to handle them. Do your research to make sure you're not going to be burdened with a dog that will cost you a lot of money in grooming bills you don't want to pay, or one that sheds her hair, if you don't want to clean up after her.

Jack Russells, for example, shed their hair and only need an occasional bath and their toenails clipped. Poodles, on the other hand, need regular trips to the dog groomer to prevent them from turning into giant canine puffballs. Whatever breed of dog you have, it's a good idea to take her to the groomer at least once when she's still young, as part of the socialization process. Give her a positive experience at the groomer's, and if you ever need to go back, she'll be conditioned to like it. Take some food with you so you can do some treat training and keep your dog's attention focused on you while she's being groomed.

Having her hair and nails clipped and ears washed is an experience unlike any other your dog's likely to have. Look at taking her to the groomer as a training exercise, and take the opportunity to accustom her to the environment and desensitize her to being touched and handled in that fashion. Otherwise, she may resist being bathed as she grows older and bigger.

Years ago, I cut some corners and neglected to properly introduce the concept of grooming to one of my dogs. By the time he was an adult dog, 100 pounds plus, he bucked like a bronco every time I tried to bathe him. It was a miserable experience for us both, and by that time it was too late for me to do anything about it. I was stuck trying to bathe him while he fought constantly to escape.

You can practice desensitizing your puppy to being cleaned at home as well as at the groomer's. Clean out her ears and wipe away any gunk that collects in her eyes. Brush her teeth. Bathe her. Shampoo her. Even if you don't plan on doing these things regularly, you're providing experiences that will make your dog easier to handle if you ever need to do them again.

Some people say that their dogs try to bite the groomer. Having her nails clipped is an odd sensation for a dog, and she may react badly. Taking your puppy when she's very young will decrease the chances of that problem arising. The groomer will thank you as well.

SHOULD I USE A DOG RUN?

Some people find dog runs valuable additions to puppy training. If you have the money and the desire to invest in a dog run, it can only be to your dog's advantage. Typically, a run is a small fenced-in area in your yard where your dog can play and explore without any risk of transgressing to places you don't want her to go.

Most runs have a concrete floor to make them weatherproof,

and some sort of cover from the rain and the sun. You may choose to put toys in the run, although not toys that you want to use for training, but instead something like a Jolly Pets Push-n-Play dog ball.

While it's a great additive to dog ownership, don't make the mistake of substituting a dog run for all the other exercises and training techniques in this book. You still need to provide your dog with focused exercise and socialization time outside the run.

A CRITICAL TIME

The first few weeks of your puppy's life with you are the times you have the greatest control over her experience. Use them to make sure your pup feels comfortable and to begin setting expectations. Time spent socializing and building a routine at this age is absolutely crucial, and will ease the process of further training. It will also help you build a relationship with your puppy. The more experiences you can give your puppy when she's very young, the more you'll desensitize her to undergoing similar experiences when she's older. Be careful, however, to avoid over-stimulating her or rushing into serious training before she's ready.

Lay the foundations well, and both you and your puppy

will be prepared for basic training during the first six-teen weeks.

3
CHAPTER

Eight to Sixteen Weeks

Basic Training

BEGINNING TO TRAIN YOUR PUPPY

When you first start to train your puppy, it's important that you keep the training fun, stress-free, and slow. Training her to walk off-leash comes later, and if you try to jump to more advanced obedience training, you'll run into problems. When your puppy is very young, you'll be lucky to make a walk last around the block. Expect your dog to randomly sit down, to be distracted by a passing leaf, to chew on sticks, to run to the right or the left, or to flop down on a bed of grass and start licking herself clean. Resist the urge to become frustrated, and realize that you're dealing with a very small puppy. At this stage, her motivation and your relationship with her is far more important than teaching her to walk on a leash.

For that reason, consider holding off on formal walks with your pup. Focus instead on building a routine to take her from the crate to the designated bathroom area, and on off-leash outdoor playtime. If you don't have access to an area where you can safely allow your dog to roam off-leash, invest in a long line or a drag line so that you can give your puppy freedom while remaining in control of her movements.

If you do decide to walk your puppy, don't try to do too much too soon, because you'll only end up curtailing your puppy's enthusiasm for being on-leash, making it harder to condition her to it later. Remember that it's not your fault if your puppy's unresponsive. She's still very young, and everything is new to her. At this stage, she's very easily distracted.

Set aside a lot of time, don't expect to get very far, and be ready for her attention to be captured by everything she sees. Keep it positive, and avoid yanking or dragging on the leash. If you need to redirect your puppy, do it gently, and be patient.

Make a very clear distinction between trips to the bathroom area, field trips to the park, and any walks that you do decide to take. You're aiming to condition your puppy to understand when she's being taken outside specifically to go to the bathroom, and when she's outside to play with you. If you don't do this, you may find that your dog dawdles when you do take her outside to use the bathroom. During Boston winters, this can be miserable!

An eight-week-old puppy won't be capable of holding off going to the bathroom in the crate for more than two or three hours, depending upon her size and breed. Her bladder is just too small. By the time your dog is a year or two old, she should be able to hold off going to the bathroom all day if necessary, but it will take time and patience to reach that stage. When your dog's a puppy, your aim is simply to condition her to be comfortable in the crate for longer and longer periods of time. Set simple goals, such as her being quiet and calm in the crate and not going to the bathroom in the crate.

To achieve this, start crate training right away. If you wait until your puppy's twelve weeks old and *then* start crate training her, you're asking for issues with barking and whining. Ideally, you want your puppy to start adapting to the crate from the day you bring her home so that she has no other point of comparison and being in her crate is simply a part of life. Dogs are extremely good at adjusting to circumstances, and they will. If you approach crate training correctly from the beginning, you won't run into many issues.

Twitch was crate trained from eight weeks old. Now she's comfortable in her crate for eight hours and beyond, without making a sound. I can drive the five and a half hours between Boston and Philadelphia with her in the back of the car, and she's quiet the entire way. At home, her crate door is open and she's free to wander inside it whenever she's over-stimulated or tired. Around nine o'clock each night, she goes upstairs and puts herself to bed in her crate. An hour later, she's curled up fast asleep. She's been conditioned to like her crate.

Older dogs that haven't had any crate training often start barking, walking in circles, and gnawing on the metal mesh when they're first crated. That's the value of crate training your puppy early.

Crate training is one of the most valuable tools in your arsenal, because it manages your puppy whenever you can't give her your full attention. If your dog's not comfortable in a crate, and you leave her at home while you're out, you'll probably come back to find that she's gone to the bathroom in the house, chewed up the couch, and barked out the window.

For most people, the biggest challenge with crate training is barking and whining. Some puppies are quiet almost instantly in their crates. Others like to bark and whine. If you open the door and let the dog sleep in bed with you, she'll quiet down instantaneously, but next time you want her to go in the crate, she'll bark twice as much.

Whenever you take your puppy out of the crate, encourage her to use the bathroom. You can do this one of two ways: either scoop her up and take her outside to the bathroom area you've designated, or attach her to a leash using a collar or harness and walk her outside.

Very young puppies have no concept of waiting, so if you leash them and start walking through the house, you may find that they use the bathroom before you can get them outside. That's a clear signal that you need to start scooping them up and taking them outside quickly, before they can go.

Monitor your dog's water intake. Some dogs will drink well past the point of hydration, which only causes them to go to the bathroom excessively. To remedy this situation, consider only giving your dog access to her water bowl at certain times of the day. The later into the evening you allow her access to water, the more opportunity she has to fill her bladder directly before bedtime, making it much more likely that she'll have an accident in the crate overnight. Personally, I pick up my dogs' water dishes at 8 p.m. You may wish to do the same. When your dog's very small, keep a really tight rein on her freedom. Don't give her free run of the house. Make her world small, and expand that world only as she gets older.

Wee-Wee Pads are pads that create a space where your dog can go the bathroom inside. The idea is that you cover a relatively large area with them at first, and gradually reduce that area until your dog is going to the bathroom on one pad in one area. They're best avoided, because they give your dog the initial message that she can go to the bathroom inside, and they create more work when it's time to change that behavior. Condition your dog to use the bathroom outside right from the start, and she'll soon get the idea.

This technique creates a clear association between being calm and quiet in the crate and being let out to use the bathroom, so be consistent. Use a long leash, and choose a spot in the yard or neighborhood that will become her bathroom area. If you let her out freely or just keep walking, she'll probably become distracted and start gamboling around the yard. Keep her on the leash and communicate clearly that she's outside to use the bathroom.

Depending upon the size of your dog, her bathroom area could be anywhere from ten to a hundred square feet, but don't allow it to get too large, otherwise the clear association will be lost. Give her three to five minutes to go. If she does, reinforce the behavior with a food reward and some playtime with you when you get back inside. If she doesn't, take her back to the crate and try again in ten or fifteen minutes.

As a rule of thumb, a puppy eating good dog food should only be eliminating as many times as she eats. If she's eating twice a day, she should be eliminating twice a day. You want her to urinate every time you take her out of the crate, but you needn't expect her to defecate that frequently. Before long, your puppy will get into a rhythm, so you'll know when you can expect her to defecate.

Feel free to reward your dog when she does what you want. When she uses the bathroom where you want her to, throw her a little party for a few seconds. Clap your hands and praise her effusively: "Good girl! Well done!" Give her a treat and some playtime with you. Make the outcome of doing what you want her to do exciting for her.

Use praise when you're playing with the dog, too, and combine it with food so that you're giving the dog a doubly positive message. You can increase the impact of playtime by making it both scarce and highly stimulating, with lots of noise and laughter.

Specifically, be sure to praise your dog whenever she comes back to you. That's a very valuable reflex, and you want to encourage it as much as you can. Back up a little and clap your hands and give her a quick scruff on the face and a scratch behind the ears. If you're already doing some treat training, give her a piece of food too. As the dog gets older, you may want to be able to recall her off-leash, and praising her when she's very young is the start of that process.

At this age, resist negative reinforcement as much as possible. Find reasons to say yes rather than no, and use the fact that you have control over your puppy's life at this point to create new opportunities to say yes. Seek to condition your dog to do the things you want her to do and, if you notice yourself saying no a lot, reevaluate how you're using the tools available to you. Is your dog using the bathroom in the house? Is she chewing things? Is she barking out the window? Return her to her crate whenever you can't give her 100 percent of your attention, and you'll eradicate these behaviors before they take root.

There is one exception to avoiding corrections at this early age. If you do take your eye off your dog for a moment and catch her in the act of going to the bathroom inside the house, clap your hands and say "No, no, no!" Quickly scoop her up and take her outside to your designated bathroom area. An effectively timed correction here will give her a clear message about what you *don't* want her to do, and what you want her to do instead. Unless you actually catch her in the act, however, there's not much you can do. If you don't realize what she's done until a few minutes after the fact, resist the urge to scold her or shove her face in it. She won't make the connection because too much time has elapsed, and you'll only be abusing her to no positive effect. Return to the foundation of using the crate effectively, create reasons to say yes, and reward her when she does what you want her to do.

TREAT TRAINING

Treat training is an excellent way to stimulate your dog's food drive. All dogs need food to survive, so they're naturally attracted to it. Control your dog's food drive, and you're already laying foundations you can use to teach her how to sit, how to go to her bed, and how to come when called. Be proactive about assessing and increasing your dog's food drive, and adjusting the food you use to train her. If your dog has a high food drive, you can use kibble as a treat and a lure. If your dog's not motivated by kibble, experiment with higher value food such as chicken, cheese, or hot dogs.

As I said earlier, chicken is very effective, although be sure to prepare it and use it separately from your own food so that your dog doesn't form an association between chicken and the kitchen table. Otherwise you risk encouraging the formation of begging behaviors.

Give your dog the smallest possible treat that she'll work for. When you give a dog a treat, she should take it, barely chew it, and swallow it, all in less than a second. Anything more than that is distracting her from what you want to achieve. Avoid anything that crumbles or is too large. A dog biscuit can take as much as fifteen to thirty seconds for a dog to crunch to pieces, eat, and lick up all the crumbs. That takes too long, and disrupts the process of training. A small piece of chicken will be snapped up in an instant, and then you can move on. Keep her attention on you, rather than on the food, by giving her a morsel and immediately offering her the opportunity to work for more.

The first technique to master is the lure. Take a piece of food and wedge it in the base between your pointer finger and your thumb. Keep it mostly covered, but leave it slightly visible so that the dog can see it and smell it. If you hold the food in a closed fist, it will seem to the dog that there's no way of accessing the food, so she'll be less motivated and more likely to give up. Stay in control of the food, so the dog can only get it when you allow her to, but make sure the dog knows the food is within reach.

You can allow her to lick it, but make sure she can't take chunks out of it until you're ready to release it.

Hold the food close to your dog's nose, and move the food around. Lure her a couple of feet in a straight line, and then exclaim "Yes!" and release the food. Practice luring your dog upwards and downwards so that she gets used to following a lure in all directions. Keep it simple at first. Give her victories. If you try to lure a small puppy thirty feet, she'll lose interest. If your lure is erratic and hard to follow, she'll soon give up. Lure her a little way, and reward her with a piece of food. You're conditioning her to work for the food, and to be confident that she'll be rewarded when she does the work.

To start with, keep the lure very close to your dog's nose. You want to provide her with maximum stimulation. The further away from the dog's nose the food is, the harder it is to lure her into the precise position you want her in. As you become more skilled at using the lure, and your dog learns to follow it, you can gradually draw it further away from her nose. That's known as fading the lure. Ultimately, you're aiming to do away with the lure altogether. An adult dog shouldn't need a lure to sit or lay down. By that time, you will have completely faded the lure and your dog should be responsive to your commands without a food reward, although you can still praise and reward an adult dog if you want to.

Of course, if you're working with an adult dog and she hasn't done basic lure training, you'll need to start where you would with an eight-week-old puppy. There are no shortcuts.

Some puppies will pick up the basics within seconds. Others may need a few days. Once your puppy gets the hang of this game, step it up and start having some fun with it. Lure her in a straight line. Lure her in a circle. Set up a mini obstacle course made of toys and chairs, and teach her to go over the toys and under the chairs. Lure her up or down stairs. If you have a yard with a children's play area, take her on the swings and down the slide. The only limit here is your imagination. You can use this technique to have a lot of fun, bond with your dog, and at the same time increase her food drive.

You can even start basic obedience training at this age. If your dog can follow a lure, start teaching her how to sit, how to lie down, how to come, how to go to her bed. If she masters those behaviors, consider moving on to tricks such as rolling over, spinning, and begging (sitting pretty). The command, cue, or name of the behavior isn't important at this time. You're only trying to shape these positions/behaviors you're putting her into.

The more training you do while your dog's very young,

the more she'll understand what you deem to be good behaviors. Aim to do a little bit of training with your puppy every single day, and avoid encouraging behaviors that you don't want to see. If you don't want your dog up on the couch, don't ever let her up on the couch. If you don't want her to beg at table, put her in her crate while you're eating.

MARKING BEHAVIORS

Marking a behavior is a way of communicating to your dog that you like what she's just done. Without markers, you'll be restricted to training your dog with just food and lures—a horse and carrot approach—limiting the extent of her training. Using markers is extremely important to seed future training behaviors, and you can start doing it early in your dog's life. The intention is to give her the message as clearly and quickly as possible, directly after she's done what you want her to, in order to create a strong association in the dog's mind between the behavior she's exhibited and the praise or reward. The more clearly she understands why she's getting the treat, the more willing and likely she'll be to repeat the behavior.

The first thing you need to do is establish a marker. Simply using the word "yes" is very effective. To start with, keep the food behind your back and walk around. Wait for your dog to follow you, which she will do if you're using quality food and she has a high food drive. For a dog that doesn't have such an intense food drive, you can tether her to your waist or hold a leash in one hand to prevent her from becoming distracted.

Your first task is to do what's called charging the marker. This is used to create an association in the dog's brain between the marker and receiving a reward. For maximum effectiveness, keep the hand you have the treat in behind your back while you're walking around. The reason for doing this is to keep your dog focused on a medial part of your body, such as your chest or face, rather than purely on the hand that delivers the treats.

After you say "yes," wait a full second, then bring your hand out from behind your back and give her the treat. The delay allows her to distinguish between the "yes" and the receipt of her treat. If you forget to leave a delay, your dog may associate the movement of your hand with the treat, rather than the verbal cue. Create a clear pause between the "yes" and the distribution of the treat.

Every time your dog does something you want her to do during your treat training session, say "yes" and give her a piece of food. This communicates the relationship between the "yes" and the reward. Enunciate the "yes" as clearly as possible, so there's a clear distinction between the way you say "yes" in normal conversation, and the way you say it when you're training your dog. The particular sound should be unique, so that your dog recognizes and understands the significance of it instantly. At first, decide what to mark using very minimal criteria. Almost any behavior is sufficient. If your dog looks in your direction or gives you eye contact, mark the behavior. If she lies down, mark the behavior. If she follows you around, mark the behavior. The only exceptions are behaviors that you don't want to encourage, such as jumping up on you, barking, or pawing at you. If your dog does any of those things, wait until she calms down, *then* mark the *desired* behavior.

Once your dog has mastered this phase of training, you can move on to marking specific behaviors by combining both luring and markers. Dogs are creatures of habit, so they'll soon form a solid association between the "yes" and the piece of food. To apply this technique to teaching your dog to sit, lure her into a sit as before and, at the moment her haunches touch the ground, mark the behavior by saying "yes" and giving her a piece of food. To attach a marker to her going to her bed, lure her to her bed, and at the moment she reaches it, say "yes" and give her the food.

It's vital and often tricky for new dog owners, to make the

sound as consistent as possible. After years of practice, I've developed a very specific way that I say "yes" that sounds almost as though I'm sneezing, and that I can reproduce whenever I need to. If you're struggling to make the sound sufficiently consistent and distinctive, you can purchase a clicker to serve that purpose for you. Every time you press the clicker, it produces exactly the same sound, which simplifies the training. The only disadvantage is that you need to make sure you remember to carry it with you if you're training outside the home. Forgetting it will render training ineffective.

Markers are an exceptionally valuable way of communicating with your dog. They also provide a lot of mental stimulation. After a two- to three-minute marker session, you'll notice that your dog is already more relaxed and less anxious. Undertake two or three marker sessions with twenty-minute breaks between them, and your dog will be quite tired, even without any physical stimulation.

All dogs are different, so there's no exact number of treat training sessions you should expect to complete in a day. If your dog has a very high food drive, she'll be motivated to practice many more times per day than if she has a low food drive. As a rough guide, aim for around three sessions per day, each lasting approximately two to three minutes and based around meal times. Doing it before she eats means she'll be hungry and motivated to work. Avoid training for longer time increments, because your dog may lose motivation if she perceives that food rewards are too easy to achieve. Instead, train in short bursts. Ninety seconds to three minutes is ideal.

Don't feel that you need to be constantly training your dog, either. At this age, she (and you) need plenty of downtime to integrate the training. That will have the added advantage of making training fun and keeping your puppy motivated to train. Always leave her wanting more.

TOY TRAINING

All dogs have a natural play drive. To foster a good relationship with your puppy, make sure you take time to play with her and teach her basic games. Some new dog owners take their puppies to the park, throw a ball forty or fifty yards away, and—when the puppy doesn't respond—assume that she's not interested in playing fetch. A young puppy has no foundation for understanding the game, and probably won't even see a ball thrown that hard and that far.

To teach your dog to play, take baby steps. Start small. Initially, keep play sessions very short: three to five minutes. To cement your relationship with the dog, make the game as interactive as possible. When you bring out a toy, you are activating it. You are making it move. You are making it tug. Don't allow your dog to take the toy and wander off into a corner with it. You want your dog to develop a strong association between you and the toy. You are the element that makes the toy fun.

To reinforce that perception, keep toys in a box or a bin with a lid on it, and only bring them out when it's time to play. If the toys become too easily accessible, you'll lose the ability to influence your dog's play drive. In your dog's eyes, you want the toys to be valuable. Whenever you bring the toys out, that's a signal that it's time to play.

If you leave toys lying around, they'll lose their power to motivate your dog. There's also a risk that your dog will start to mistake other household items for tug toys, and develop a chewing habit. Keep sessions short and pay attention to your dog so that you know what games she likes. Playing with you should feel like a treat to your dog. Be willing to try different toys to find the ones your dog responds to most enthusiastically; it'll depend upon your dog's breed and individual temperament. Some dogs enjoy playing fetch with a tennis ball. Others prefer a tug toy. Still others are more interested in rolling around on the floor with you.

There are a few exceptions to this rule. You can leave

a Nylabone out, because it's a chew toy only. You can leave a KONG out for the same reason. Anything that you activate and that you're using to develop your dog's play drive should be kept under lock and key.

A tired puppy is a happy puppy, and a happy puppy leads to a happy owner. Give your dog ways to play and run and enjoy herself while connecting with you or with other people or dogs. Does she love playing tug? Give her a game of tug after you take her to the bathroom and before you put her back in her crate. Does your next door neighbor have a dog? Introduce them and let them play for a few minutes. Does your dog like going to the park? Take her out and let her chase you, or play any other game you both enjoy. When you bring her home, she'll be in a relaxed state of mind, and you'll be able to leave her in her crate for a few hours.

Neglect exercise, however, and your puppy will become restless and anxious in her crate. Dogs need a physical outlet, and if you don't give it to them they'll be frustrated and agitated. It's very difficult to crate train a puppy that's not getting enough exercise, and it increases the chances that she'll become destructive when she *is* out of the crate.

Typically, you'll either be playing some kind of tug game or some sort of fetch game. If you're playing with a tug toy, keep it attached to a string or a leash. That keeps the game interactive and prevents your dog from taking the toy to her crate or into a corner of the room and chewing it until it's destroyed. That's a natural impulse, but it's not helpful to you in training your dog. Use the string or the leash to condition her to bring the toy back.

A good routine is to toss the tug toy and let your dog jump on it. Wiggle the string or the leash so that the toy moves, providing extra stimulation for the dog, and start to reel it in, quite slowly, until you have the toy in your hand. At this point, pet your dog and give her some praise. Allow her to tug with you for the toy. Withdraw and give your dog full access to the toy for five to ten seconds. Then, clap your hands, pat yourself, and encourage the dog to bring the toy back to you voluntarily. You're conditioning her to see you as the source of the toy and to bring the toy back to you on command.

Another option is to keep your puppy, rather than the toy, on a leash. As long as either the toy or your dog is under your control, you're establishing good playing habits. Some breeds of dog are more likely to run away with the toy given the chance, so assess your dog's temperament when deciding whether to leash her or the toy.

Keep sessions very short at first: between three and five

minutes. The higher your dog's toy drive, the longer sessions can be. For a dog with low toy drive, make sure that you're ending sessions while she's still excited so that next time she'll be ready for more. The moment your dog's interest in the game is peaking is the perfect moment to end it.

Another good game is running around outside holding a piece of food, and having your dog chase your lure. When she reaches you, give her a piece of food and switch direction, so you're running the other way as quickly as you can. She'll start to chase you again. The moment she reaches you, give her another piece of food.

Controlling your dog's toy drive gives you the foundation you need to take command of her when she's off-leash later in life. Feasibly, it could even save her life if she's in a dangerous situation and you need to bring her back to your side. I've conditioned Twitch to value one particular toy exceptionally highly. As soon as I bring it out, she flies to my side instantly and I have total control of her. That makes it possible to take her off-leash even in downtown Boston, with cars, squirrels, skateboards, other dogs, people, and numerous other distractions. As long as I keep the toy by my side, she's glued to me. That's how powerful a strongly conditioned toy drive can be.

Playing with a ball also works well. Again, attach it to a string to keep the game interactive and maintain control. If your puppy takes the ball into a corner and you find yourself chasing after her to get the ball back, you're not really training your dog; your dog's training you. Keep the ball game within an enclosed area to limit the potential for your puppy to give you the runaround, and consider having a second ball on hand to regain your puppy's attention if she becomes too focused on the ball and not focused enough on you. Take a second ball out and bounce it a couple of times, and it's highly likely your puppy will drop the ball she already has and come after the ball you have.

Always remember that you are the game maker. You activate the toy. Without you, it's dead. As your dog grows older, you can use the principles described here to give her high intensity exercise. Ten minutes of fetch, played at full pelt two or three times a week, is worth more than three hours of walking seven days a week and will have a more positive effect on your dog's overall state.

For an even more effective routine, combine mental and physical stimulation. Take time to train her to sit, or walk up the stairs, or come to you through a homemade tunnel, using a lure. Mental stimulation tires dogs out almost as much as physical stimulation. Make sure that by the time you put her in her crate for the night, she has a reason to be tired and ready to rest.

I started playing with Twitch when she was ten weeks of age. The first game was tug. She learned when to let go of the tug toy and when to pick it up. That expanded into games of fetch, where I'd throw the toy about three to five feet, back up, and clap my hands. When she brought the toy, we played tug. When I told her to drop it, she dropped it, and I either threw it again or immediately re-engaged in playing tug.

Over time, that evolved into fetch. I use a Chuckit! toy—a plastic arm with a cup at the end, which can launch a ball fifty or sixty yards. After ten minutes of playing with the Chuckit!, Twitch is exhausted. She wants nothing more than to go home and lie on her bed.

Play games like this with your dog and you'll build a fun and harmonious relationship. You'll be able to exhaust her whenever you want, which is vital. An under-exercised dog is an anxious, barking dog. You'll also have a lot of fun yourself. At fourteen months, Twitch can chase a Frisbee and pluck it out of the air. She can dive into the water to chase a toy. That all started with very short games of tug.

Consider finding a way to get your dog involved in agility

training or sports. If you have a bird hunting dog, such as a pointer, look for a local club. Exercise your dog correctly, and you'll give her a sense of purpose, foster her confidence, and give her vital physical stimulation.

Playing with toys is preferable to wrestling and roughhousing with your puppy, because the latter may encourage her to use her teeth more. Roughhousing is fun, but there's no real training benefit. That said, the temptation to get down on the floor and wrestle with your dog can be strong. My dog Ripley loves to wrestle. Understand, however, that if you roughhouse with your dog, you're conditioning her to become mouthy, and she may be developing bad behaviors.

While you never want your dog to nip at you, it's important to realize that very few dogs will bite out of the blue. If yours does, look at the reasons and take steps to prevent a repeat. Evaluate how you're playing with and stimulating your dog. Is her excitement level getting out of control? Most dogs will nip only when they become over excited, or because they're receiving stimulation that triggers a bite reflex. Some owners play by pushing the dog or grabbing the dog's face. Those types of play will trigger a reaction and could result in a bite. Before you criticize your dog, take a look at your own approach and ask yourself what you might be doing to cause the nipping. Your dog reflects your energy, and you have more control over her than you might think, especially when she's very young. Use a toy as a mediator, so if your dog bites, she will bite the toy rather than you.

If your dog bites you during a game, simply end the game. The fun stops, and you calmly redirect the situation. Stand up, put her on a leash and take her outside for a bathroom break. If she's still rambunctious, scoop her up or lure her into her crate for a cooling off period. You're not punishing your dog; you're simply bringing an end to the stimulation that led to over-excitement.

Many people worry that they'll create a negative association in the dog's mind about being crated, but that's only the case if you respond aggressively. If your dog nips you and you react by holding her mouth shut, grabbing her by the scruff of the neck, and throwing her into the back of the crate, she will undoubtedly come to associate being in the crate with punishment. That can lead to problems with crate training, and the stimulation of the dog's defense drive. Keep doing this, and before long your dog won't be biting because playtime got out of hand. She'll be biting in an attempt to defend herself.

Your aim is to de-escalate the situation and casually bring the dog's energy level down. Give her time to chill out. A tendency to bite or nip is easily discouraged at a young age, and for a small puppy, all you need to do is stay in control of the situation and bring the energy level down.

USING PRAISE

Along with food drive and toy drive, make sure that you're building your dog's drive to receive praise from you. The best way to do this is to combine praise with more tangible rewards, such as food and playtime, before gradually transitioning into using praise alone.

When you praise your dog, show her that you're genuinely excited and happy with her. Really explode with praise so that she gets the message loud and clear. At the same time, pet her and scratch her behind the ears—anything to let her know in the strongest possible terms that you're happy with what she did. Talk to her as you'd talk to an infant—raising your voice, clapping your hands, and whooping and hollering with enthusiasm.

Make sure that moments you're praising your dog contrast very clearly with moments you're not praising your dog. Be generally calm and casual, and when they do something you're pleased with, erupt with joy and happiness. After a couple of seconds at that peak, return to a calm state and continue as normal, until the next time you want to praise her. The greater the distinction between praise and non-praise, the more clearly your dog will understand that you like what she's doing and which behaviors you're seeking to reinforce.

TERRITORIAL AND DEFENSE DRIVES

Along with food drive, toy drive, and praise drive, your dog will have other drives that you don't want to encourage. The most common, and some that can easily become problems, are territorial and defensive drives. Wolves in the wild are very territorial, and even domestic dogs retain those instincts.

Every dog will have different drives in different proportions. Good protection dogs, for example, should have a much stronger defense drive than lapdogs. Be prepared for your dog to display these drives so that you know what's happening when she does and you don't become concerned. The worst mistake you can make is to bury your head in the sand and hope that your dog's anti-social behaviors will go away of their own accord. You can't completely eradicate territorial and defensive drives, but you can certainly desensitize your dog to the stimuli that trigger them and increase other drives so that you can override them.

Let's assume that your dog has a very high defensive drive

and keeps barking at people that come into the house. Work on increasing her food and toy drives so you can lure her back under your control and redirect her whenever she starts barking. If her food and toy drives are high enough, her attention will be instantly diverted from being territorial and defensive to playing or eating.

Most Belgian shepherds have a naturally high defensive drive, which is bred into them to protect stock. Without training, Twitch would be at risk of developing a propensity for barking and charging at people. Her toy drive is so high, however, that I can easily override her defensive drive by bringing out her favorite toy and redirecting her to her bed, into a down position, or just generally focused on me.

The exception is protection dogs, which are bred and trained to have higher defensive drives. For the average household dog, however, a high defense drive is more of a nuisance and a danger than an advantage, and you'll want to minimize it to prevent problems. It should be possible for a guest to enter your house without triggering a fierce reaction in your dog.

Once your dog is a little older and comprehends motivation through negative reinforcement, you can start to apply pressure to reinforce the message alongside food or toys for redirection. If you use corrections or say "No!" as your only method of training—for instance, start yelling at your dog when she's already stressed and in a defensive mindset—you'll make the behavior worse. Always seek to redirect your dog and de-escalate the situation using food or a toy before you start correcting this behavior.

HOW TO DISCOURAGE BEGGING

Some people like to have their dogs at their feet while they're eating, because they enjoy the companionship. If you do that, however, you need to understand that there's a high chance that your dog will smell the food you're eating and start to beg. She will become conditioned to being around you when you're eating, especially if you reward her begging with food, or even accidentally drop scraps every now and again. Reversing a begging habit once it has taken root is quite difficult, but preventing begging in the first place is relatively easy.

To prevent your dog from begging at table when she's older, establish a routine of feeding her directly before you sit down to eat. For maximum effectiveness, feed your dog in her crate. This will create a positive association for your puppy; her crate becomes the place where she gets her survival needs met, and this will avoid the complication of her associating your kitchen table with high value food.

Do this, and you'll cut off the possibility of begging before it even takes root. Your dog won't be around you while you're eating, so she won't ever pick up scraps that get dropped accidentally. She won't ever learn that there is a possibility of receiving food from the table. The crate becomes a tool that you can use to take begging out of the equation.

Once your dog gets a bit older and her ability to follow commands improves, you can send her to her bed during meal times and expect her to stay there until you say otherwise. Resist the temptation to take shortcuts, however. An eight- to sixteen-week-old puppy might be able to go to her bed when told, but expecting her to stay for more than a few seconds is asking a lot, especially when there's food on the table. Once a dog approaches the table and starts to smell food, she'll naturally be stimulated and want to eat. Keep your dog away from the table while you eat, and the problem will never develop.

DISCOURAGING JUMPING

To discourage your dog from jumping up on people, increase the strength of other behaviors. Once your dog sits or lies down on command, you can override her impulse to jump up on people by redirecting her towards positive behaviors. If you increase your dog's food drive using the feeding technique and luring described earlier, you can easily get her attention when she starts to jump up on people by bringing out some treats and luring her into a sit or to her bed. Alternatively, use a favorite toy to redirect her when she becomes fixated on a guest. Your aim should be to redirect her energy onto you and the toy rather than on jumping and climbing onto your guests. The more control you have over your dog's drives, the more easily you can redirect her behavior when she's exhibiting traits you want to discourage.

If your dog's jumping up on other people who come into the house, leash her and step on the leash so she has enough room to move but not enough to jump. Combine that with luring the dog into a sit, and you'll very quickly convey the message that jumping on people is not good and sitting brings a reward. This technique is equally effective when you encounter a passerby while out on a walk.

Another tactic is to stay very calm with your puppy for a few minutes when you first come home or take her out of her crate. If you've been out of the house, even for half an hour or less, she'll be very excited to see you. The same holds true if she's been in her crate for a couple of hours and you let her out. At this point, don't encourage her excitement. Don't get down on the floor with her. Don't clap your hands or praise her. Simply put her on a leash and take her out for a bathroom break. If you mirror her energy when she's highly excited, her excitement will become even more intense, to the point where she won't be able to contain herself from jumping up on you. Present a very calm energy and expect her to understand that it's time to be calm. She'll soon learn.

If your dog has already started to jump, there are things you can do to correct her. As always, however, it's better to prevent the behavior than correct it. You can use your knee in a sideways motion, so that as your dog jumps you swipe sideways and push her away from you using your knee against her flank. Don't push your knee straight into her head or chest, and minimize the impact as much as possible. The aim is to redirect her and return her painlessly to the ground, not to punish her. Another option is to hold both her front paws until she tries to take them back. This will panic a dog slightly, and when you let go of her paws, she probably won't want to jump up again.

Always opt for positive methods, and absolutely refrain from being aggressive towards your dog. If you scold or yell at your puppy, you may eradicate the behavior you want to discourage, but at a huge cost to your relationship with the dog. Teaching your dog not to jump up is an important part of the socialization process. Invite people into your home and encourage the dog to greet them but not to jump up on them. Be consistent in your approach, expect your puppy to learn good manners, and she will.

INAPPROPRIATE BARKING

Dogs bark for many reasons. They bark to get attention, because they're anxious, because they're territorial, restless, or need physical stimulation. Often, barking is an expression of a dog having too much energy and no outlet for it.

The lower and more sporadic a dog's bark, the more defensive they are. If your dog has her butt in the air and her front feet down with a high pitched bark, that's a playful bark and stance. If she has her tail down between her legs and her ears back, that indicates avoidance and fear. A dog with her tail and ears straight up confidently paired with a rhythmic bark is a bark out of prey drive, typically when she's anticipating play with a toy. Get to know your dog so you can assess the reasons why she's barking.

A few people *like* their dogs barking, but the vast majority want to control it. If your dog is barking and you want her to stop, try giving her some exercise. Play tug with her for a few minutes. Throw a ball in one direction and, when she reaches it, throw another ball in the opposite direction, so she's constantly chasing after one or the other.

Mental stimulation is another way to quell inappropriate barking. Practice some treat training, luring your dog into a sit and marking the behaviors you want to encourage. Give a restless puppy something to focus her energy on, and she will lose interest in barking.

Some dogs bark when they see or hear people moving around outside, or when someone knocks on the door or rings the doorbell, because they're territorial or anxious. Once again, the key is to redirect your puppy. Give her something else to focus on. Increase the level of physical activity you're providing. The trick is to increase your dog's food and play drives to such an extent that you can get her attention even when her defensive and territorial drives are stimulated. This takes time and practice, and it's a reason why the training foundations are so important. Without them, you won't be able to take control of your dog's drives when you want to.

Nine out of ten dogs respond very well to squeaky toys. If you want a sure-fire way to get your puppy's attention, you can buy a squeaky toy, remove the squeaker, and keep it in your pocket. Whenever you want your dog to focus on you, hit your pocket and your dog will be instantly captivated. That's an excellent time to lure her into a sit or into lying down.

A word of warning, however: don't try to distract your

dog from barking by giving her food before you've redirected her attention. If you do that, you'll be inadvertently rewarding the behavior you want to discourage and creating an association in your dog's mind that when she barks, she gets food. For the same reason, don't try to soothe her or pet her while she's barking. Many people think they're soothing the dog's anxiety by doing this, but actually they're praising and encouraging the barking. Think redirection, not soothing.

If you're one of the small percentage of people who *does* want your dog to bark when people come to the door, encourage your dog by tapping her side in an agitated manner and speaking to her in a suspicious and anxious tone. Exhibit a little anxiety yourself, and work her into a state where she'll bark. Instead of seeking to calm and redirect her defensive and territorial drives, aim to stimulate those drives. For the vast majority of dog owners, however, I highly recommend avoiding this technique.

BE CONSISTENT

Dogs thrive on consistency and predictability. If you tell your dog to get off the couch one day then allow her on the couch the next day, you'll confuse her. The same is true of crate training. To condition your dog to the crate, you need to send out a clear signal that you expect her to be calm and quiet in there, and hold to that expectation.

It's okay to change your strategy if something's not working, but do so in a way that's consistent with your overall goals. When Twitch was very small, her crate was downstairs, and she whined in the night and sometimes went to the bathroom in her crate. I brought her into my bedroom and, whenever I heard her whining in the night, I reached out, said "hey...hey...hey" in a calming voice and simultaneously gave her three quick little taps on the crate to redirect her and remind her that everything was okay. She soon learned to calm down and sleep soundly in her crate. Be willing to adapt your strategy, but don't abandon the crate or your other goals altogether.

Owning a dog is work, and to train your dog correctly, you need to make absolutely sure you can devote the time required both to crate train her and to give her the physical and mental stimulation she needs. It may seem a lot of effort at first, but by the time your dog's one or two years old, you'll be able to loosen up the discipline and enjoy the fruits of your labor.

SIXTEEN-WEEK MILESTONES

Many people wonder what stage a puppy should have reached by sixteen weeks. While every dog is different, there are a number of milestones to aim for, all of which are achievable in this timeframe. You can use this section as a checklist to assess your puppy's progress and to highlight any areas you need to work on.

By the time you've had your puppy for two months, she should be comfortable in a crate for about three to four hours at a time during the day. Episodes of barking and whining should be decreasing in frequency, and your dog should be feeling increasingly at home. As long as you're not keeping her in the crate too long, your pup should be fully potty trained, with accidents in the crate a thing of the past. She should be sleeping overnight in the crate, in whatever location you've found works best for her.

By sixteen weeks, you should have a clear idea of your dog's temperament and an understanding of situations in which she's comfortable and situations in which she becomes stressed. To do this, you'll have taken her to a range of different environments—at least four to six—with different levels of stimulation, and observed her responses.

Food and toy drives should be increasing, and you should have a solid feeding routine established, using foods that she likes and that are healthy for her. You should know what her favorite toys are. Your dog should be conditioned to follow a basic lure to sit, lie down, and go to her bed.

You should be marking behaviors, either with a "yes" or with a clicker.

If all of those behaviors are in place, you're right on track. If not, you know where to make adjustments. The next step is to expand the training, adding challenges and refinements as you go.

CHAPTER 4

Sixteen to Twenty- Six Weeks

Building on the Foundations

EVOLUTION, NOT REVOLUTION

Dog training is based on progression. When you and your dog are comfortable with the milestones listed at the end of the last chapter, you're ready to move on to the next phase of training, even if your dog is younger than sixteen weeks. If she's still struggling to follow a lure or having accidents in the house, despite having reached sixteen weeks or older, she's not ready. Keep working on the basics until you're comfortable, and make sure you have a solid foundation. Accept that, if this is your first time training a dog, it may take longer for you and your puppy to master the foundations. That's perfectly okay.

You can expect your dog to be more confident and secure by this age, as long as you've been observing her temperament and responding accordingly. She will be more settled in her crate. You'll have taken her to meet a range of people, in a range of environments, and had an opportunity to assess her level of comfort. You'll have a good idea of what she can handle and any situations that cause her stress. This is a good time to start taking a shy dog to slightly more stimulating environments, helping her overcome her shyness, while always being careful not to overwhelm her. Handle her well, and you'll notice her becoming more independent. By now, she should feel like part of the family.

Continue socializing your dog and broadening her repertoire of experiences, and at the same time start leaving her in the crate longer between bathroom breaks. By this stage, your puppy will have formed some conception of holding in her bladder and bowel movements rather than releasing them immediately, especially if you've been consistent in the times you've taken her outside. Her bladder will also have increased considerably in size, giving her a much greater capacity to wait.

Start increasing the time between bathroom breaks. If

your puppy has been going to the bathroom every three hours, aim to up that to four hours, then five. A lot depends on the breed of dog here, because larger dogs have bigger bladders and can hold it for longer. Cut out some of the regular bathroom breaks. A small puppy may need to use the bathroom as many as ten to twelve times in a day. As she grows, you can reduce that to eight times, then six, and soon you'll have successfully house trained her.

By this time in your puppy's life, you should have been able to diagnose any major concerns about her bathroom behavior and take steps to eliminate them. Have you noticed her going to the bathroom in the house? If so, you know to control the time she spends out of the crate more, and take her outside as soon as you let her out of the crate. Does she need to use the bathroom too frequently? You can check how much water she's drinking, and adjust if necessary. Any flaws in your pup's schedule should be apparent by now, allowing you to take action to remedy them.

By this age, your dog's food drive should be noticeably higher than it was when you brought her home. Continue encouraging her to eat her food promptly, and take the food away after a few minutes if she doesn't. The same should be true of her toy drive, and her coordination will be sharper.

In summary, this is a time to take your puppy's training to the next level, and also to take a step back and look at any problem areas. Is she still jumping up on people, or onto the couch? You can see which areas of your puppy's training are going well, and which need some work. Territorial and defense drives will kick in more strongly, too, so if there's work to do on preventing your dog from barking or growling, you'll notice it. She's becoming more lively, more engaged, and more stimulated by life.

Don't be tempted to abandon the training or the crate at this point. This is a time to build on the strong foundations you've already put in place. Many people crate train their puppies from eight to sixteen weeks, then put the crate in the basement and think the dog is crate trained. It takes a lot longer than that to fully condition a dog to be comfortable in her crate.

This phase is an expansion of the previous one, a time to take stock of what's working and anything that isn't, and tweak your approach as your dog grows.

EXPANDING OBEDIENCE TRAINING

Sixteen to twenty-six weeks is an ideal time to start working obedience commands into your training. Up until this point, you haven't been using commands all that much, and if you have, your puppy is still primarily complying because of the food. You've been relying and focusing on luring the dog where you want her to go, and marking the behavior by saying "yes." Now you can take the next step.

At this point training becomes more functional, with more real world applications. You're conditioning your puppy to follow your commands so that, ultimately, she will be able to do the same on- or off-leash in challenging places.

When you lure your dog into a sit, add a command. Any command will work. I taught Twitch in French and Ripley in English. Some people use Chinese or Spanish. Your dog will understand any word as long as she can associate it with the desired behavior. So, if you're using the word "sit," issue the command as you lure your dog into a sit. Do the same with other commands, such as "lie down" and "go to your bed."

Again, make sure that the command is distinctive enough from your normal patterns of speech that your dog can clearly distinguish when you're giving her a command and when you're having a conversation.

Continue using a lure, but start fading the lure further from your dog. You may be able to hold the lure a foot away from the dog's nose, or have the lure at your chest.

Recognize your dog's capabilities and work progressively. It's vital that you sustain her interest, even if that means holding the lure closer to her nose than you'd like.

To teach your dog to sit, lure them into a sit as you have done previously. *As you lure*, issue whatever command you want her to recognize as "sit." When her haunches touch the ground, mark the behavior with a "yes" and give her the piece of food. At this stage, make sure that you are adding a command every time you use a lure.

Another important aspect of training at this stage is to incorporate an implied "stay" into all commands. When you first begin obedience training with your puppy, she won't hold the behaviors for very long. She may sit when you lure her into a sit, or go to her bed when you lure her there, but as soon as something distracts her attention, she will get up and do something else. Sixteen to twenty-six weeks is a good time to start changing that.

To instill the concept of an implied "stay," start by integrating it into your "sit" command. To do this, lure the pup into a sit as above, and then take one step back. If she stays where she is, mark the behavior with a "yes" and give her a piece of food. Take a step to the left. Again, if she stays, mark the behavior and reward her with a piece of food. Repeat moving to the left and right, backwards and forwards. Whenever she stays where she is, mark the behavior and give her a piece of food.

At first, your dog will probably move as soon as you do. Be patient with her. Return her to exactly the same spot, lure her back into a sit, and try again. You're sending her a clear, consistent message that if she sits, she gets a "yes" and a piece of food, whereas if she moves, she doesn't get a piece of food and she has to start again. A young puppy will probably find this very challenging. Take any opportunity to mark the behavior and reinforce your expectations.

You can use a light "no" marker when she does get up, but keep the training as positive as possible and don't get frustrated. Give your puppy as much success as you can. If necessary, take smaller steps: half a step back or to the right, instead of a full one. Staying while you step back is easier for the dog than staying while you step to the right or left, because she can remain focused on the food. To make it easier for your dog, experiment with raising your arm as you step to the left or right, holding out the hand with the food in it and keeping the food directly in your dog's arc of vision.

From here, build the implied stay into every command you teach your dog so that it becomes a natural part of her training and she learns to wait patiently wherever she is.

RULES OF PLAY

Sixteen to twenty-six weeks is a good time to introduce a stronger training element into play sessions. The way to do this is to strengthen the rules of play.

Toys stimulate dogs very differently from food. Food stimulates the dog's food drive, because she knows she needs food to live. Toys, however, combine elements of play and prey to get her into a state of motivation called high drive. When your dog is in high drive she will give you 110 percent of her attention. To do that, you'll need to enforce a few rules.

The first rule of play is always to have control of the game. When you first bring a tug toy out of the box or shelf, attach your dog to a leash. A four-, six-, or fifteen-foot line will work. It doesn't really matter. By attaching your puppy to the leash, you create a game where carrying the toy off isn't allowed or even possible. Most puppies will try to take the toy off on their own simply because it's valuable to them. Leashing your puppy also allows you to play these games outside where being off-leash is not an option yet.

The second rule is to build your puppy's drive and confidence for the game by giving her tons of victories. A lot of dog owners are under the impression that they should never let the dog win. This might be the case for extremely dominant dogs, but for 99 percent of dogs out there, let them win, a lot. Never letting your dog win is a sure way of minimizing your dog's toy drive, rendering toys completely useless for training.

To let your dog win, simply back up and present the toy to your dog. Make sure the way you're holding your toy doesn't block the puppy's access to it, otherwise she may accidentally chomp on your fingers. As your pup takes hold of the toy, gently wiggle it back and forth, making it seem alive for a few seconds, then release the toy to your dog. As she carries it and holds the tug, encourage her to bring the toy back to you by backing up, clapping your hands, and making sounds that you know she likes. Try to avoid pulling her on the leash if you can. As soon as she's close to you, let her know that you're not interested in taking the toy away. Petting and praising her enthusiastically adds to the pleasure of being near you while she holds the tug. You can also take hold of the toy with a slight grip, wiggle it a couple times, but then let your puppy have it again.

One of the biggest reasons why a dog carries the toy off, won't bring it back, and refuses to let it go is because each time her owner gets near her, the toy is taken away, in some instances, forcibly. Condition your puppy to become comfortable around you while she has possession of your toy.

The next rule for your puppy to learn is to drop the toy when asked. The best way to introduce this idea without decreasing your dog's toy drive is to use food. I recommend chicken. When you're ready to have your dog release the toy, hold it calmly and say "out" while simultaneously touching a piece of chicken to her nose. In the dog's mind, you're not really taking the toy away as much as you're simply making an exchange for it. After your puppy releases the toy, mark the behavior "yes" and let her have the piece of food. After she's finished eating the treat, get another game of tug started.

Like all behaviors, the "out" command is taught progressively. First, say "out" while touching her nose with a piece of food. The next step is to say "out," THEN give her a piece of chicken after the fact. Lastly, you'll start rewarding the "out" behavior by simply re-engaging in the tug game. As soon as she releases the toy, mark the behavior "yes" and reward her with the toy. All methods condition your puppy to realize how great it is to release the toy.

All toy training ultimately comes down to those two factors: bringing the toy back to you and letting it go. When your dog's older and you're playing fetch in the park, those are the behaviors you want her to exhibit. You want her to bring back the ball and let it go so you can throw it again.

Here are some pointers while teaching your puppy the rules of play:

- Bring a lot of energy to the game. Half of the fun is playing with you! Without you, the toy is just a random piece of cloth, rubber, or synthetic material. The toy is dead, and it only comes alive when you hold it. Since you'll be very animated and energetic, make sure you have enough space to play tug. Playing tug outside for this reason is great. However, be sure that distractions are limited, because you want your puppy to focus on the session and not redirect to another person, dog, or object.
- Avoid letting your puppy chew on the tug. Remember that your goal is to use these rules of play to train your puppy, which means this toy is a reward. A reward toy is different than a chew toy, so I encourage owners to use them as they were designed to be used.
- Puppies usually chew on the tug toy if they're given the opportunity to lie down with it. Keep your puppy moving. Back up, clap your hands and gently pull the lead towards you if you need to. In order to keep control of the toy, your puppy will have to hold it more firmly instead of chewing it. If/when she drops the toy because she's fumbling around or chewing it, keep moving backwards away from the toy. Hold your puppy on-leash with one hand, and reach down and pick up the toy with the other. Then start playing tug again. By doing this consistently, you'll condition your puppy to hold the toy instead of chew it.

- Keep sessions relatively short. I encourage owners to end the tug session at its peak. Leave them wanting more. Depending on your dog's drive and the temperature outside, sessions can range from ninety seconds to close to ten minutes. Shorter sessions will create more drive for the next session.

- Don't rip the toy out of your puppy's mouth. You'll not only hurt her mouth and maybe damage a tooth, but also strip her of her confidence in her ability to play tug.

- Some puppies are silent and some are very vocal while playing tug. I advise owners to diminish growling as much as possible. Growling and vocalization in general is usually stimulated as a product of over-zealous tugging. If you aggressively shake the tug, you'll notice your puppy growls more. Try to avoid this by tugging more gently or not tugging at all, and simply pat your dog when she's holding the toy. Dogs will reciprocate your energy, and if you tug hard and erratically, so will they.

- When you're "outing" your puppy (training her to release), shift your energy. By shifting from a playful tugging and boisterous energy to a dead, still, unresponsive energy, you'll eliminate a lot of your puppy's desire to tug on the toy. Don't wiggle or move the toy, otherwise you will stimulate your dog to want to tug. Calmly hold the tug and "out" your dog (issue an "out" command). Then, when you're ready to start tugging again, become animated and fun.

- Try tugging with other toys such as a ball, Frisbee, or maybe even a water toy. This will make the game more interesting and also transfer to different sports as she grows older. To play tug with different objects, you may need to fasten a handle, rope, or leash to the toy so that you can tug it without damaging a finger.

Your aim is to use the toy as a way of motivating your dog in obedience. At a more advanced level, you can use the toy itself as a reward. For example, when your dog sits successfully, you play tug with her for a few seconds. You issue an "out" command, she drops the toy, and you practice another behavior, such as lying down or rolling over, followed by rewarding her again with a few seconds of play. This only works if she is conditioned to drop the toy when you command her to. Otherwise, you may reward her with the toy, only to find that she grabs it and runs off with it, leading you, the owner, to come on *her* command.

DISTRACTION TRAINING

Another way to add intensity to the training is to incorporate distractions. Judge carefully when your puppy is ready for more distractions. Don't make the training more complicated while she's still struggling with the basics.

When she's comfortable with basic commands, you can take her outside into somewhat crowded areas and test her ability to follow those commands while distracted by stimulation. Try insisting upon a sit/stay when someone enters the house, or while greeting another dog, even if only for a split second. While walking your puppy on-leash, work on sitting at crosswalks. Conditioning your dog to obey commands while she is distracted will prove invaluable as she grows older.

Consider enlisting your family to help train your dog to sit and stay when a family member enters the house. Send your partner or one of your children outside for a minute or two, and practice the sit and stay commands as they return. Aim to hold the dog in a sit for ten seconds, and then allow her to get up and play.

Don't expect your dog to be perfect at this point. Give her lots of help and realize that she will still break the commands. As long as she's getting better from day to day, that's enough.

A basic sit command, along with "lie down" and "go to your bed," will help you redirect any bad behaviors your dog is developing. If she's jumping up or barking out the window, work on making the bed command strong enough to override those impulses. When you have people in the house, take the opportunity to strengthen the commands by working on obedience in a distracting environment.

As your dog becomes more accomplished, you may start to fade out the use of food in training, but only a little. Many people attempt to fade out the use of food too quickly, and diminish the dog's motivation. Reward at least two out of three behaviors with food, and the third with genuine and enthusiastic praise.

It's important to keep in mind that at this stage your expectations that your puppy sit, lie down, and go to her bed on command, along with practicing an implied stay, are confined to your short training sessions. As she gets older, you'll apply the training more and more broadly. For now, however, keep sessions very short and upbeat. Remember to limit them to around two to three minutes each, and aim for three sessions per day.

LEASH TRAINING

Before your dog is sixteen weeks old, she won't really benefit from being taken out on a leash. As mentioned in previous chapters, you can take her out on a harness, but don't expect to get very far. Around sixteen weeks, however, your puppy is capable of walking much further and doing so without the number of breaks and distractions that you'd expect of a younger dog. This is a good time to stop using a harness and transition to a flat collar. In fact, the majority of training time at this stage should be on-leash, so that your dog gets used to the sensation of having a collar around her neck and being gently redirected with a tug on the leash.

Harnesses are designed to distribute the weight of any pulling the dog does. I use a harness for Twitch when I'm working on protection exercises with her. The reason for this is since she's pulling so hard, a small and restrictive collar would choke her and ultimately discourage her from pulling towards her target. For normal walking, however, you *want* your dog to feel pressure when she pulls at the leash. That's partly how she will learn not to pull.

There are a few exceptions. Sled dogs wear harnesses because they're pulling an enormous amount of weight and they need to distribute it as widely as possible. Protection dogs also benefit from being encouraged to pull. If you have a reason to encourage your dog to pull, stick with a harness. Otherwise, transition to a flat collar.

You can attempt the switch cold turkey or work more gradually. Either switch out the harness for the collar or attach two leashes to your puppy, one on the harness and one on the flat collar. In this way, your puppy will only be getting half of the pressure of the flat collar. Once she's comfortable with the flat collar, you can eliminate the harness altogether. This transition can take anywhere from minutes to a week or two.

An excellent exercise for training your dog to walk on a loose leash is to take her to a relatively low stimulation environment and tether the leash to your belt with her either on both the harness and flat collar or just the flat. This will keep your hands free and allow you to focus on proper luring and distributing high value treats to captivate her attention. Walk around the low stimulation environment and casually change direction from time to time. Every single time the dog looks at you or moves towards you, mark the behavior with a "yes" and give the dog a piece of food while you continue to move; also, as your dog looks at you or moves in the same direction as you, say "heel" or the command you want to associate with loose leash walking.

You want the dog to walk on a slack leash. When she does that, say "yes" and give her a piece of food. Whenever she starts to pull at the leash, stop and backpedal. You don't need to turn around completely. Just walk backwards until the dog stops pulling away from you and gives you her attention. Then mark the behavior with a "yes" and give her a piece of food.

Essentially, this is the introduction to negative reinforcement. Pressure on the collar is added when there's tension on the leash then subtracted when the leash is loosened. The negative reinforcement is the subtraction of pressure on the collar.

The area needn't be large. You can walk in a big circle, or stake out a 20 x 20-foot piece of land, and practice walking back and forth within that space. Be sure to mark any time your pup is walking beside you on a loose leash, and reward her with a piece of food. As soon as you feel tension on the leash, reverse until the leash is loose again, then reward.

This is an extremely important step to conditioning your dog to walk on a loose leash, and it's the ideal time to do it, before she becomes too large or the habit of pulling on the harness becomes too ingrained. Most dogs that pull have been conditioned from a very young age and developed an expectation that they will feel tension on the leash. They don't feel comfortable walking on a loose leash because it's an unfamiliar experience for them, as if they were floating off into space.

It may only take your dog a few days to become comfortable walking on a loose leash. It may require the entire period between sixteen and twenty-six weeks. However long it takes, start to introduce distractions as she becomes more proficient. If you have a child, ask the child to come out into the yard while you practice, and provide some extra stimulation. Your dog will naturally gravitate towards a new person, giving you an opportunity to back up and mark the behavior with a "yes" and a piece of food once the tension on the leash stops. Try throwing a ball and rewarding your dog for not chasing the ball, or going to a place where there are other dogs and rewarding her for staying on a loose leash.

The higher your dog's food and toy drives, the more effective this exercise will be. You're aiming to be more stimulating, in your dog's eyes, than whatever attracts her attention in the moment. The easiest way to do that is to have something the dog desires, be that a piece of chicken or a favorite toy.

Some dogs will adapt to walking on a loose leash very quickly. Others will take more time and may be affected by particular types of stimulation. Read your dog, and shift your focus accordingly. If she's distracted by other dogs or by cars, introduce them to her slowly. Start this process now, and eventually she will be able to walk off-leash and stay focused on you even when something highly stimulating, such as a squirrel, crosses her path—but that will take time.

Should your dog exhibit any bad behaviors during the training, such as growling at other dogs, keep a squeaker in your pocket that you can use to redirect her. Continue to build her food and toy drives, and use those to return her attention to you whenever it strays. Once again remember that, for now, your expectations that your puppy will walk on a loose leash are confined to short, two- to three-minute training sessions, three times per day, and in an environment with minimal distractions.

RECALL COMMAND

Conditioning your dog to come to you when called is one of the most important pieces of training you can do. It's very useful when you're outside or at the park with your dog while she's off-leash. When you're ready to leave, you simply call her to you, put her in the car, and go. In more extreme circumstances, being able to recall your dog on command could save her life. Imagine your dog off-leash on a busy street and seeing something that catches her attention—a squirrel or a ball or a leaf blowing in the wind. If you can't bring your dog back to you with a command, there's a chance she will run into the road and get hit by a car.

Choose your command carefully because, like other commands, you want it to be a sound your dog doesn't hear on a regular basis. It needs to be distinctive enough to spark her attention. When training Twitch, I used "Ici!" which means "Here!" in French.

You also want to make sure your recall command is short,

catchy, and sharp. It's the command you'll be using over the greatest distance, so the more aurally stimulating it is for your dog, the better. When I say "Ici!" it's with an extended first syllable, at a high pitch. "EEEE-ci!" That sound is powerful enough to instantly catch Twitch's attention from fifty or sixty yards away, even if she's playing with another dog, and bring her flying towards me. Some people use a whistle instead of a vocal command, which also works well.

The recall only becomes truly functional when your dog's old enough to be taken outside off-leash, but you can start laying the foundations between sixteen and twenty-six weeks. Practicing a restrained recall, which is the first step, requires two people, so you'll need someone to assist you.

Start with your assistant physically restraining the dog, keeping a tight hold on her so she cannot get to you. Select a piece of high value food and approach the dog, bringing the treat right up to her nose so she's stimulated by the smell. Move your hand around a little so that she's stimulated both by the smell and by the movement. Doing this activates both her food drive and her prey drive. They should be very activated and engaged.

Step backwards a short distance, about five to ten feet. Give your recall command, which is also the cue for your assistant to release the dog. When your puppy starts to move towards you, mark her first step with a "yes" and keep walking backwards, rewarding her with the treat when she reaches you.

Later on, you'll want to add what's known as a finish to the recall, which is the action you want your dog to take when she reaches you. If you reward her by holding the food between your legs, approximately level with your knees, it will be very easy to add the finish at a later date. You're conditioning her to come to a position where she can lie down, spin to the left, spin to the right, run between your legs, or do anything else that you want her to do. Consistently rewarding your dog right at your knees lays the foundations to bring her as close to you as possible and brings her to the same position whenever she reaches you.

A lot of owners reward dogs haphazardly, sometimes giving them treats with the left hand, sometimes with the right, other times dropping or throwing the treat. Sometimes people walk towards the dog, which slows the dog down and decreases the effectiveness of the command. Some people lean forwards and give the treat as the dog approaches, which conditions the dog to stop a few feet away before reaching the owner.

The most effective choice is to keep moving backwards to

continue stimulating your dog's prey drive and allow her to move towards you faster, conditioning her to run at great speed towards you when you give her the recall command.

Say "yes" only once, to mark the dog's first step towards you. Psychologically speaking, you're marking the dog's decision to come towards you. Once she's moving, and her food and prey drives are activated, she won't require any further encouragement. Over time, however, start to fade the marker so that you're saying "yes" later and later. Move from marking the first step to marking the second step, then to marking the third step, and so on. Eventually, you're marking the moment when she reaches you and sits in front of you, or does whatever else you want her to do. Over time, you'll be able to fade the lure completely, and call her to you using only your recall command.

Developing a strong recall takes a lot of practice. Start around sixteen weeks, and initially stay in an environment with very few distractions. Develop the command inside the house or in the backyard before taking it into more stimulating environments. Make progress gradually from being five or ten feet away to being twenty or twenty-five feet away. You want your dog to have a consistent experience of coming towards you 100 percent of the time when she hears your recall command, which is why you start small. She should rarely, if ever, have the experience of hearing the recall command and not come towards you.

That's the reason for beginning with the restrained recall. A dog that sees you with a piece of high value food five feet away will come towards you without any other encouragement. As she does that, you're familiarizing her with your recall command so that, later, when you're thirty feet away, or in another room, or up the stairs, the association between the command and coming towards you will be exceptionally strong.

You can usually release the restraint within a few days, as soon as your dog makes the association between your recall command and coming towards you. When you're confident that your dog is ready, progress to a free recall. For this, your assistant releases your dog and allows her to investigate whatever catches her interest for a few seconds. When you're ready, issue the recall command, mark the first step as she comes towards you, and reward her with a piece of food when she reaches you. Only do this when your dog's responding to the recall command every single time while restrained, and when you're sure she will come when called. If she's captivated by a smell at the other side of the room, or by a favorite toy, don't dilute the command's effectiveness by using it and not getting the response you want. Control the environment so that you know you'll be able to call your dog successfully.

It's important to keep challenging the recall command so that you can build a high level of trust between you and your dog. Ultimately, you want to be able to recall her in high distraction environments from long distances, but reaching that point is a gradual process of adding in more distance and more distractions over a period of months.

An excellent way of doing this is to set targets during outings. For example, once the command is strong, decide that you'll practice three recalls during a trip to the park or a friend's barbeque. Allow your dog to play and enjoy the environment, and at three distinct points during the course of the outing, issue the recall command and expect your dog to turn instantly and come barreling towards you.

A barbeque or party is a high stimulation environment, with food, other people, probably children, other dogs, and a whole host of smells. To recall your dog in that situation, your recall command will need to be so strong that it's an automatic, conditioned response for her to come to you whenever she hears that sound. This is also a perfect illustration of why your recall command needs to be distinctive, to penetrate your dog's ears in an environment with so much noise and other competing stimuli.

By this age, you should notice that your puppy is starting to like her crate. She should be much more accepting of the time she spends in there, with no resistance.

She should be more confident and secure in a range of different environments, even if she was initially apprehensive. This includes making canine friends, whether that's one dog at a time or a few, depending upon your pup's temperament. She should be relatively comfortable around other dogs and, if she's not, you should be able to discern patterns and pick up on any cues that might lead to trouble.

The same goes for people. By this age, your dog should have been introduced to a wide range of people of different shapes, sizes, and colors, wearing a range of different outfits. You should have a good idea of your dog's relative level of sociability, and be able to adapt excursions accordingly. If you've taken your dog to an event with a lot of people, you should have an idea of how relaxed she feels around many people. Did she waltz around comfortably, or did she hang back with her tail down? If necessary, you should be applying solutions by taking her to different environments where she's more comfortable.

Obedience training at this point in your dog's life will still be taking place primarily in very low distraction environments. She should be able to sit, lie down, and go to her bed, either without using a lure or with a lure that's faded quite far from her nose. She should know the recall command, and any other basic obedience commands you're teaching her, and be able to follow them with little or no luring. She should understand the concept of an implied stay, and be able to stay for ten seconds and beyond in an environment with minimal distractions.

Distractions will occur, however, and you shouldn't expect your dog to be as responsive while distracted as she is in a controlled environment. A dog that can sit without a lure when there are no distractions may need a lure when someone knocks on the door or walks past the fence. You'll need to lower your expectations to accommodate the effect of distractions and work gradually to a point where your dog is very responsive to you even in a distracting environment.

By twenty-six weeks, your dog should be more than halfway trained. She'll be getting more proficient at obedience training, and you should be much more confident in your ability to train her effectively. At this time, a lot of people are happy with the level of training their dogs have reached. If that's you, congrats and kudos. However, if you want to take training to the next level, you'll need to introduce a new form of motivation—motivation through the use of negative reinforcement. During the next phase of training, you'll begin to solidify and proof your obedience behaviors, add more and more reliability to your commands, and at the same time eliminate bad manners that may have formed.

5 CHAPTER

Six to Fifteen Months

Introducing Corrections

PROOFING THE TRAINING

All the techniques you've been learning until now have been reward-based. Once your dog reaches around six months of age and you're comfortable with the previous phases of training, we begin to make a slight shift. It's time to add the element of motivation through negative reinforcement, or the removal of something unpleasant.

Many people, particularly in the United States, object to the idea of using negative reinforcement in their training regimen. They view prong collars and electric collars as a last resort, the bigger stick, and refuse to use them. In other parts of the world, such as France, Germany, or

England, these collars are known as training collars, and are simply accepted as a necessary part of training.

If you want to teach your dog a functional and reliable recall command, one that will hold even from a distance in public places where distractions are at their highest, you will need to sharpen her training using either or both of these collars. Ninety-nine percent of dogs need some level of negative reinforcement to strengthen their training to the point where their behaviors are totally reliable.

The more effectively you've laid the foundations in previous phases of your dog's life and training, the less you'll require negative reinforcement to proof your training. If you follow the exercises in previous chapters of this book, your dog will have a high food drive, a high toy drive, and a solid understanding of basic commands. You will have a good relationship with your dog, she will be motivated to do as you say, and she will require only minimal corrections to her behaviors. Without a strong foundation, this new way of training won't be nearly as useful, so be sure that you and your dog's understanding of the basics are down pat.

A dog that has been trained primarily using a reward-based system in her foundational work will be far more bold, confident, and will completely dominate and even welcome the negative reinforcement you're about to layer in. As you slowly introduce prong or E-Collars into her training cycle, it's very important that her motivation and engagement is high. Used well, negative reinforcement becomes a great motivational tool. Dogs soon understand that they control the adverse stimulation and not the other way around. This creates trust, predictability, and in turn, reliability within the behaviors—all while retaining the highest level of motivation.

Never teach your dog a new behavior using corrections. They are a latter step, not a first step. This is an advanced alteration to your dog's thinking and should only be implemented on top of a SOLID foundation. Many people attempt to reverse the order, and hurt and confuse their dogs. The most common misuse I come across is how owners use it for the recall. If you attempt to teach your dog the recall behavior with a weak or nonexistent foundation by simply strapping on an E-Collar, calling your dog, and then correcting her when she doesn't come, you will more than likely confuse her. If your level on the collar is too high and your timing is off, you might over-correct her and she will associate the correction with something completely different than what you intended. Ultimately, you'll give your dog an extremely unpleasant experience, and the next time you attempt to put the collar on, she'll make a break for it. The most negative impact through incorrect usage of negative reinforcement is creating apprehension and phobias in a dog's behavior and in her environment. Not knowing when and where the corrections are coming from will riddle a dog with insecurity and anxiety. Only integrate negative reinforcement into training once your dog already knows the behavior you wish to proof.

SHOULD I USE CORRECTIONS?

Imagine this scenario. You're in a field doing recall training with your dog, and she's doing very well. You're using a high value treat such as chicken, and when you call your dog, she comes directly to you. Now, what happens if, as your dog turns towards you, she sees a squirrel? Will your dog continue towards you, or will she take a detour and head off towards the squirrel? If she will obey your command despite the distraction, then why complicate life? However, if she will veer off towards the squirrel and having a reliable recall is important to you, consider using more advanced tools such as an electric, remote, or field collar.

This is an extremely common story. It's very hard to compete with the stimulation of a squirrel, even with a highly desirable treat. You may have better luck with a coveted training toy but will more than likely still lose that battle.

If your dog will come to you when called nine times out of ten, but you lose her when a squirrel or a rabbit catches her attention, motivating your dog with negative reinforcement through the use of a remote trainer is the best way to improve the difference from nine times out of ten to ten times out of ten.

Again, this assumes that you want or need an unbreakable behavior of your dog off-leash. If you're comfortable with your dog chasing squirrels or rabbits, you'll more than likely find this process unnecessary.

INTRODUCING A PRONG COLLAR

A prong collar has a number of contacts on the inside that fit snugly around the dog's neck, toward her head. Many people fit the prong collar too loosely around the dog's neck so that it falls down towards the dog's chest. That's an incorrect fitting and will result in the prong collar not dividing up the pressure proportionately or in the right area to begin with.

The contacts on the inside of the collar constrict when there's tension on the lead, which applies pressure to the dog's neck. When the lead is loose again, the pressure is released.

When you first introduce a prong collar to your dog, fit

her and allow her to wear it for a few weeks before you start actively introducing corrections. She probably won't have any experience of wearing something metal around her neck, and allowing her to get used to the collar before you start issuing pressure gives her an opportunity to familiarize herself with the new tool. If you fit the collar and instantly begin applying that pressure, your dog will probably form negative associations with it and may react against it. Begin putting the collar on at random intervals and engage in a treat training session. Your dog will soon associate the training collar with a reward.

Other times, bring out six or seven high value treats moments before you attach the prong collar, and place them on the floor in front of your dog. As she moves along the line of treats, fasten the collar around her neck. Consider playing games and reinforcing the rules of play while the dog wears the prong collar, without issuing corrections. The more positive experiences you can give your dog while she wears the prong collar, the better for her and the better for her training. When I take the prong or electric collar out, Twitch runs over to me and sits, because she associates it with going outside to play or train. If you navigate this stage skillfully, your dog shouldn't exhibit any avoidance of wearing the prong collar.

After a couple weeks of familiarizing your dog with the

prong collar, you're ready to move on to the next phase and begin applying pressure.

WHICH PRONG COLLAR?

There's only one brand of prong collar that I recommend. It's called the Herm Sprenger, and it's made in Germany. It's the only brand that truly works and lasts. You'll find Herm Sprengers at good quality pet shops or online. Avoid store-brand prong collars from the large pet chains, which usually bend out of shape and end up breaking.

The sizes on prong collars relate not to the collar itself, but to the grade of the contacts. For most dogs, the best grade will be either 2.25 mm, or 3 mm, although smaller sizes can be used on larger dogs, and vice versa. For a dog of between five and thirty-five pounds, the 2.25 mm is probably the most appropriate size. For dogs of thirty-five pounds and above, the 3 mm size works better.

Some prong collars are quick release, while others have a standard release. Deciding which one to use is a matter of personal preference. Quick release prong collars are slightly more complicated and take a little longer to become familiar with, but are easier to put on and take off once you get the hang of it. Standard release types are simpler but require a little bit more dexterity in your fingers.

Once you've chosen a prong collar and your dog is comfortable wearing it, you can start using it to proof your training.

In a low stimulation and relatively distraction-free environment, try this simple exercise to begin proofing your sit command. Using two leashes—one on the dog's prong collar and the other on her flat collar—use a few lures and start by warming your dog up. With zero tension on the leashes, lure and ask her to sit, and when she obeys, mark "yes" and treat. Lure and ask her to lie down, and when she obeys, mark "yes" and reward her. Get her engaged and prime her to respond to training stimuli. Take at least thirty seconds to get her excited.

When you're ready to start using the prong collar, lure your dog into a sit and, at the same time, apply slight pressure upwards on both leashes, elevating her head and bringing her haunches to the floor. The moment her haunches touch the floor, mark "yes" and give her a piece of food while immediately relieving the pressure. Pressure on the leash should be done with a slight tugging motion. Aim for one or two tugs per lure/behavior. When you tug on the dog's lead, it's very important that she stay engaged and motivated to work, so apply the intensity of your pressure accordingly. All dogs are different.

The same principle applies when you're adding negative reinforcement or corrections to the down command. Use a piece of food to lure her into lying down, and as you do so, tug gently at the leash a couple times, down and off to the side. When she reaches the desired position, mark the behavior with a "yes" and give her a piece of food.

To begin adding the prong collar to the go-to-bed command, start a few feet from the bed, lure her towards it, and tug gently on the prong collar in the bed's direction. As she heads towards the bed, remove the pressure, mark the behavior with a "yes," and give her a piece of food once she's reached the bed.

The main goal of these particular exercises is to introduce our dogs to the concept of negative reinforcement, the removal of something unpleasant. We are not teaching her to sit. We're not teaching her to lie down or go to her bed. She learned that long ago. The more she understands that she controls the pressure and how to turn it off, the more successful the training will be. Her understanding of this exercise directly relates to her level of motivation. If she doesn't understand, you'll begin to notice lack of motivation.

Keep sessions short and always have a high value reward, whether it's food or a toy. Through repetition and consistency, she'll begin to understand that once she completes the commanded behavior, the pressure of the collar stops and at the same time she receives a high value reward. The more experience she has, the more confident she'll be, so do her a favor and practice this for at least a few weeks before advancing.

WALKING WITH THE PRONG COLLAR

The prong collar makes an excellent tool for training your dog to walk calmly on a leash. Once again, limit distractions severely when you first take your dog out for a walking session on the prong collar. If there are too many distractions, your dog will attract too many corrections, and the experience will become stressful. Your dog will start to lose motivation, and the point of the exercise will be lost.

I highly recommend using two leashes when you first use the prong collar outside for a loose leash walking session. In this regard, you can determine exactly when to administer pressure to the prong and when to back off. One leash should be attached to the dog's prong collar and the other to the flat collar.

If your dog is veering to your left side, your tugs on the prong will be to the right, slightly across your body. If she's veering to your right, the opposite is true. All of your tugs should target the leg you want your dog to walk next to. When your dog is in front of you, you'll be tugging her gently backwards. When she's behind you, your tugs will be forwards. For the first few walks with a prong collar, this is enough. Keep sessions short, three minutes max, and also have rewards in the form of food or a toy on hand.

Really pay attention to how you can use the second leash, which is attached to the flat collar, to control the pressure of the prong collar. At first, consider a 50/50 ratio of pressure. Then 60/40 in favor of the prong collar. Over time, the goal is to transition to the prong collar completely.

As your dog becomes more proficient at this basic technique, you can start to incorporate more distractions and longer sessions. To do this, take your dog for a short walk and be very disciplined about keeping her attention focused on your leg. If she sees a squirrel or something else that catches her attention, do your best to stay calm and tug her gently back into position. The walk needs to be short to avoid correcting too much and creating stress.

Now is also a good time to start working on sitting and lying down outside using the prong collar, and incorporating it into other exercises. For example, if your dog is barking out the window, start layering in the prong collar to proof your bed command, which will begin to reduce the barking.

TEACHING STAY WITH A PRONG COLLAR

Whenever I train, I use an implied stay, which means that a dog will stay in one position until she's released from the behavior. When you give your dog a sit command, she should sit until you release her or tell her to do something else. The same is true of any other command. Making a stay command into a behavior of its own adds an unnecessary additional layer of complexity.

To proof an implied stay command using a prong collar, start with the exercise above and lure your dog into a sit while attached to the leash and prong. Once she responds consistently to this command, which should be very quickly if you've followed the instructions in earlier chapters of this book, STOP tugging on the leash to bring her to a sit, and revert simply to telling her to sit. You've trained her using a lure, a command, a marker, and a collar, so by this point simply telling her to sit should be enough.

While she's seated, start to walk around her in a horseshoe pattern. If she gets up, immediately (within a fraction of a second) give her a couple of tugs on the leash to activate the prong collar, command her into a sit again, and keep walking. When she stays in the same position, mark the behavior with a "yes" and allow her to come to you to receive a treat. To strengthen the conditioning, simply repeat this process. Whenever she gets up as you move around her, tug at the leash and command her back into a sit. Whenever she successfully stays seated, mark the behavior with a "yes" and reward her with a treat. Make sure you give her victories when she does what you want her to do.

The reason for moving around her is to add an element of distraction. Until they're well trained to sit, most dogs will start to move as soon as the owner or trainer does. For this reason keep the criteria for rewarding your dog minimal at first. If she stays for three seconds while you take a single step back, that's enough. Over time, expand the criteria, but don't rush. Wait an additional second, or take a step to the right or left as you move backwards. Every time your dog maintains an implied stay, reward her with a "yes" and a treat. Before long, you'll be able to stand at the end of a fifteen-foot line for a minute or two and expect your dog to stay.

As she progresses, you can make the distractions more and more pronounced, so that you're making a full circle, side stepping abruptly, or even skipping around her. Use the same principles to attach an implied stay to other behaviors, such as lying down or going to her bed. Once she's mastered this stage, work in more and more distractions by taking her out to an environment with other people and dogs.

A good correction should bring your dog back to the position you want her in, while also retaining her drive and motivation. By now, you should know your dog well and be able to gauge how sensitive she is. You can use that as a guide to how much pressure you should apply. If you have a highly sensitive dog, give her very light corrections. If your dog is more stubborn and thick-skinned, you may find you need to be a bit more assertive.

When you correct your dog's behavior too harshly, she'll yelp, wince, or otherwise externalize the correction. This means that she is only registering the discomfort and focusing the majority of her attention on the fact that you're correcting her. This is very distracting and can lead to demotivating your dog. On the other hand, if your dog continues getting up despite your corrections, your corrections may be too slight.

INTRODUCING AN ELECTRIC COLLAR

Do you need to use an electric collar? Your choice will be determined by whether you want to get control of your dog off-leash. To do that, you'll need to incorporate the electric collar into training, beginning from approximately ten months of age. Conditioning properly with an electric collar is the only way to retain control with 100 percent reliability.

If you decide that you won't ever need to let your dog off-leash in crowded or distractive areas, or you don't think you'll ever want to have your dog 100 percent under control while she's off-leash, you can forego using an electric collar.

The electric collar becomes indispensable, for example, if your dog is at a distance and you need her to respond to your voice under the influence of heavy distractions. From far away, a lure/reward or a prong collar is ineffective. You need to use an electric collar to gain control of your dog remotely.

The concept of the electric collar is very similar to the prong collar. Your dog must already have a very solid foundation in the behaviors you're seeking to reinforce *before* you start using the electric collar. The collar allows you to apply pressure to your dog using electrical stimulation operated from a distance. Don't start training with an electric collar until your dog is comfortable, responsive, and understands the dynamics of negative reinforcement through use of a prong collar.

It's extremely important that your dog has an understanding of "on and off" pressure as described earlier. She also needs to associate the electric correction with what you intend her to do, otherwise she will become apprehensive and confused. If your timing is off, she may associate the stimulation with any behavior she was exhibiting at the time, and develop phobias. For example, she may connect receiving a correction with stepping on a grate or brushing up on a trash can. You need your dog to understand that she controls the stimulation of the collar in the same way she already does with the prong collar.

A good electric collar will offer a broad range of stimulation levels. A bad one will have very few. Fifteen to twenty years ago, it was standard for a collar to only have three levels of stimulation: low, medium, and high. Those aren't enough choices. With only three options, you'll always be over- or under-correcting your dog. Look for a collar that has at least 100 different levels of stimulation.

Compare a collar with only three levels of stimulation to one with 100. I'm particular about a brand of remote collars called Dogtra. If low stimulation on the former is equivalent to level one on the latter, medium stimulation on the former is equivalent to level fifty on the latter. So, with a good collar, you can adjust the level of stimulation far more effectively. The lowest setting will be too low for almost any dog, but on a good collar you can manipulate the stimulation up to level four or five for more sensitive dogs, as opposed to ratcheting it up all the way to level fifty. If your dog is less sensitive, you can use a level in the region of twelve to twenty instead of boosting the power all the way up to a high level. Being over-corrected is a very intense experience for a dog.

Before you apply the collar to the dog, test it on yourself so you understand the level of stimulation. People who've never experienced an electric collar, or who have only felt an electric fence correction will always refer to its activation as a shock. Once they've tried it for themselves and had it explained to them, they understand why I use terminology such as stimulation, pressure, or correction instead of zap, shock, or stun.

Just as you did when you started using the prong collar, be certain that your dog understands the commands you want to proof and that she has a solid foundation in all the previous phases of training. An electric collar isn't a panacea. If you haven't played the puppy recall games in previous chapters or worked through the exercises where you allow your dog to wander off and then recall her, your recall command won't be effective by simply strapping on an E-Collar. In fact, without a foundation in recall, you'll more than likely teach your dog to run away from you when she's corrected remotely instead of towards you. Always create a bridge between one style of training and the next so that your dog understands what you're teaching her and recognizes the new rules of the game.

The first time you use the collar, keep the stimulation low, around three to eight on a scale of 100. You don't want to provoke a stress response in your dog. You want her to notice and acknowledge the stimulation but overcome it because of her drive for food, toys, or praise. When they receive stimulation from an electric collar for the first time, most dogs will cock their heads or scratch briefly at their necks where the collar is. That's how you know they've felt it and you're working at the right level.

Initially, keep your dog on-leash so you can physically move her around as she gets used to the new stimulation, and introduce the electric collar to her sit routine. Sit is such a basic and useful command that it's a very effective way of introducing any new training. Prepare your dog by stimulating her at your chosen level for one to two seconds, then tug her into a sit position while saying "sit." At the moment her haunches head towards the ground, cut off the stimulation, mark the behavior with a "yes," and reward her. Be careful only to mark with "yes" when she is fully seated.

This approach has a number of advantages. Your dog

will barely feel the stimulation, so it's not disturbing or upsetting for her. She already knows the behavior well, so she can easily absorb the added stimulation. You're rewarding her by marking the behavior and giving her food or a toy, so she gets to have a positive experience and sustain motivation. You're also conveying to your dog that she's in control of the stimulation. When she exhibits the behavior you want from her, you subtract the stimulation.

Naturally, you can apply this approach to any other behavior you want to proof using the electric collar, such as lying down, going to her bed, or responding to a recall command.

Take the transition slowly, and move step by step. Start as you did inside, by giving your dog a second or two of stimulation, issuing her a command, and releasing the stimulation when she does as you say. This may take anywhere from a couple of weeks to a couple of months. A very good sign is when your dog starts to obey the command before the one or two seconds is up. At that point, you can be confident that she understands what you're communicating to her.

Once your dog has mastered this and understands that she is in control of the stimulation, move on to giving her a command and only stimulating her if she doesn't obey in a timely manner. You're flipping the dynamic so that, instead of teaching your dog how she can turn off the stimulation, you're teaching her that she will only receive stimulation when you need to correct her.

As with other phases of training, keep distractions low to non-existent at first so that you know your dog will do what you want. It's so important that you give your dog plenty of victories in the early phases of introducing a new form of training, to keep her motivated. If you start in an environment with too many distractions, there's a chance your dog won't do what you intend her to do, and then the objective of the exercise is lost.

The next phase is to begin incorporating the implied stay with the remote collar. To do this, tell her to sit, lie down, or go to her bed. Don't correct her as she gets into the position. Just as you did with the prong collar, start walking around her. If she breaks the command and begins to get up, re-issue the command and give her stimulation from the collar on a low setting until she begins to revert back into the position you put her in. When she does, release her from the behavior with a "yes" and reward her with a piece of food. If she's confused or distracted, you can also help her with leash pressure.

The next step is to take your dog outside and intro-duce her to using the electric collar in more distracting environments. Start by attaching a long line or a drag line to your dog's prong or flat collar. During this phase, you can't be certain that she will respond to your commands or the electric collar as you wish, and if you don't have her attached to a line of some sort, you risk losing control of or even endangering her if you're in surroundings where she could run into the road. If you can, seek out a fenced area where you can be sure that your dog will be safe. Bring plenty of food with you, and a toy that you know your dog loves, so that you have a few different tools at your disposal in case you need to redirect your dog's attention back to you.

Your aim is to gradually build distance between yourself and your dog, and to proof commands such as sit and lie down, both incorporating an implied stay. Think of the electric collar as an invisible leash that you can use to redirect her when you need to. If your dog would be tightening a physical leash, or is venturing beyond the boundaries within which you're training her, you need to convey to her that the electric collar functions the same way a leash would. When her attention starts to wander, she will feel stimulation and you will redirect her attention back to you, just as you would if she were attached to a leash. Soon, you will begin to phase out the use of a leash by dropping it and letting her drag it behind her or removing it altogether. You may not be physically tethered to your dog while you're using an electric collar, but the bond is just as strong as if you were.

It bears repeating that you must *never* attempt to teach your dog a new behavior using an electric collar. This phase of the training is a very small percentage of the total time you will spend training your dog, and you must not skip over the rest of the training to reach this stage and expect to be successful. An electric collar is an advanced tool, for use with trained dogs only. This is the most complex technique in this book, and it requires a sound knowledge of your dog's temperament and a solid relationship with her.

Every dog reacts differently to the electric collar. I have a range of basic electric collar lesson plans, but it takes all my experience to adapt those for the numerous different ways in which individual dogs respond to stimulation. If you're struggling to get it right, don't flounder in the dark. You'll probably confuse your dog and damage your relationship with her. Call in a professional who can teach you how to use the collar effectively.

The electric collar is an excellent tool for gaining full control of your dog. I use it for all my dogs, and it makes the difference between a dog that is 90 percent trained and one that is 100 percent trained. That said, I'm very aware of the stigma the electric collar has, because I see so many people misusing them and causing harm. Only use one if you need to gain control of your dog off-leash, and make sure that you train your dog effectively before you do.

ENJOYING YOUR DOG

By the time you've completed all the exercises in this book, your dog should be fully socialized and house trained. She should have mastered basic obedience commands. Depending upon how far you've chosen to take the training, she may be capable of playing Frisbee in the park with you, going off-leash, and coming back to you on command. You'll have not only a loving companion, but also a well-trained, immaculately well-behaved dog that is a pleasure to be around and can be introduced to friends and family members without concerns that she will cause problems.

There are no limits to how far you can take training. If you've ever seen footage of a dog show or a range of dog sports, you'll have an idea of what's possible, and that's without even considering dogs that have been trained to bring their owner's slippers, fetch toys from the lake, or do any number of extraordinary things. While this book only covers the basics, the techniques contained here will prepare you for any additional training you might wish to take on. Otherwise, kick your feet up and enjoy the relationship you've created with your dog. Congratulations!

Conclusion

A Trained Dog

BEYOND FIFTEEN MONTHS

Once you reach your goals, you can relax your dog's training a little. Before your dog is fifteen months old, put her in her crate whenever you leave the house, even if it's only for a few minutes. If she reaches that age and you're confident that she won't go to the bathroom in the house, chew on anything, or cause any other problems, experiment with allowing her out of her crate while you take a short trip to get something out of your car or to the mailbox, then even longer trips like to the grocery store. Give her a toy, such as a KONG filled with peanut butter or yogurt, to chew on while you're away.

Expect your dog to be in roughly the same place when you return. That's a good sign that she's calm and not roaming around the house in search of something to chew on. As the months go by, gradually prolong the time you leave your dog alone. If she regresses, don't go back to square one. Shorten the time you leave her alone, and make sure she has something to play with. Try freezing the peanut butter in the KONG because it will hold her attention for longer. Alternatively, look at interactive toy games that present your dog with a puzzle to solve to earn treats. The Wobbler is a good one. It's a top-heavy toy that you fill with treats. As your dog whacks away at the toy, it dispenses treats slowly, a few at a time. Also, make sure your dog is good and tired through intense exercise.

Did you decide at the beginning that you wanted your dog to eventually be allowed on the couch? Now's the time to lay a blanket on a specific area of the couch and teach her a place command. Allow her to relax and get used to her new circumstances, and redirect her if she moves off the blanket. Consider leaving the crate door open so she can come and go freely. Most dogs, once conditioned to their crates, will happily sleep there and will prefer it to other locations.

Don't change the rules forcefully. If your dog wants to continue sleeping in her crate, don't insist on anything else.

If she doesn't show any interest in getting on the couch, don't make her. In your eyes, she may have completed her training and deserve to "graduate," but that doesn't mean she'll understand that concept or want to do things differently. Nonetheless, this is the point at which you can broaden the scope of your dog's options and freedom, knowing you can always bring her back to her training if she ever oversteps the boundaries.

Dogs live to be ten, twelve, fifteen years of age and beyond. If you train them properly for the first two years, you'll reap the benefits for the rest of their lives. You can take them for walks, on or off a leash, and know that they're under control and giving you their attention. You can trust that they've established regular eating and bathroom routines. Having a trained dog is a wonderful experience. Having an untrained dog is difficult, challenging, and frustrating.

A FINAL RECAP

Now that you've finished reading this book, it should be clear that training your dog is a progressive process. Start with the simplest aspects, such as housebreaking and socialization, and you'll be able to transition smoothly into more advanced training step by step. Neglect the basics, and you may succeed in teaching your dog tricks, but she won't be well adjusted and fun to be around. It's so much harder to work backwards and reverse engineer the behaviors that you want your dog to exhibit than it is to get it right the first time.

If your training routine is well planned and effective, each step will flow naturally from the previous one. Pavlov's dog experiment is well known, but few people recognize how significant it is for the average dog owner. Everything you do is conditioning your dog. The more consistent you are in your expectations and your training, the more responsive your dog will be. An effectively conditioned dog will remain quiet in her crate until you let her out to go to the bathroom. She will go to the bathroom quickly and go to her crate while you feed her. She will eat her food within a couple of minutes. If you condition your dog well, you won't even need to ask her to do these things. She will do them automatically.

Take a moment to review your goals for your dog and think about your strategy for achieving them. Are your goals and your strategy coherent? Are you teaching your dog to do the things you want her to do when she's older? You can use your goals as a reminder and a checklist in case you ever lose track of what you're doing with your dog and why.

Some people think that training dogs suppresses their natural instincts, but in fact it's the most effective way of harnessing those instincts for their benefit and yours. A trained dog is a highly motivated, happy dog. You have four primary tools to motivate your dog: food, toys, praise, and pressure/negative reinforcement. Always think about how you can motivate your dog to want more of what you're giving her, because your dog's drives are the greatest training tool you have.

The greatest mistake you can make when training your dog is to humanize them. It's vitally important to recognize that dogs learn differently from humans. Treat your dog like a dog rather than a human. Motivating a dog is different from motivating a human. Praising a dog is very different from praising a human. Teaching your dog new behaviors is a very different process from teaching your child new behaviors. The vast majority of problems people run into with their dogs comes from humanizing them and inadvertently encouraging bad behaviors. Always remember that you are the human and your dog is the dog, and you need to take the lead in determining which behaviors are acceptable and which are not, as well as communicating clearly through the way you train your dog.

The worst scenario, if you fail to do this, is that your dog will realize its dominance over you. Depending upon the dog, the consequences can range from the annoying to the tragic.

Don't think that you need to be a strict authoritarian, constantly belittling your dog and asserting yourself on her, but you do need to be in control of the things she needs. You control her food and water, her freedom, her access to toys and praise. She comes to view you as the source of the good things in her life, the necessary things in her life, and that gives you the authority to train her and expect cooperation from her.

Once she's fully trained, your dog will be a joy to look after and a loyal companion for life.

THE JOY OF A WELL-TRAINED DOG

I'm a canine trainer, but at heart I'm a boy who loves dogs. Different dogs have different characters. Some are highly independent, others are much more affectionate. Some like to be glued to their owners' sides.

The theory behind training is universal, but each individual dog has a unique temperament. A lot of dogs have their own quirky behaviors, such as chasing their tails or barking in specific ways. Ripley likes to stand between my legs then lean to one side and nudge one of my legs as an indication that he wants a butt scratch. When you train your dog well, there's more chance that you'll see the quirky elements of her character.

Taking a trained dog out in public and to events becomes a real pleasure. Nowadays, despite having quite a shy temperament, Twitch is comfortable in all sorts of social situations. She's also an extremely beautiful dog who never fails to attract attention. I take her to barbeques, parks, and into the city, and people always want to pet her and give her food. It brings a huge smile to my face, watching other people interact with Twitch and knowing that she's enjoying it.

A trained dog is extremely impressive to watch, a lot of fun to handle, and a lot of fun to show off to friends, or even to strangers in the park. Trained dogs are extremely sharp and extremely motivated. You can also take them to many places that you can't take an untrained dog, such as running, hiking, or camping. They will form relationships not only with you, but also with members of your family and other people in your life.

Watching Twitch and Ripley, I feel immensely proud and happy of the dogs they've become. Of course, I also feel sad sometimes. A dog's lifespan is much shorter than a human's, and Ripley is already nine years old. Letting your dog go is an inevitable part of owning one. Training is a way to maximize the highs of owning a dog and minimize the lows. The more proactive you are in your training, the more you will instill the manners you want to see—the crate training, the socialization, a sense of obedience and control, and everything else you want to see in your dog—and your dog will become an enormous source of joy and happiness in your life.

Appendix

Frequently Asked Questions

What if my dog is reacting to other dogs on-leash?

This is a problem that usually stems from a combination of temperament, lack of proper socialization, and taking shortcuts in training. If you have an adult dog and she's already exhibiting this problem, you may need to consult a professional dog trainer. You can, however, work on control exercises. Teach your dog a simple sit command, a lie down command, and train her to walk on a leash. Start inside, with very few distractions, and work towards bringing in distractions and other dogs.

If your dog can't sit, lie down, or walk on a loose leash

with no other dogs around, there's no prospect whatsoever of her remaining under control when she's stimulated by another dog. While corrections are necessary in this instance, don't use them as your primary tool to get your dog under control. That could make her more reactive. Increase her drives and learn how to properly motivate her. She needs to learn some simple commands so that you can bring her under control and bring her anxiety level down.

My dog is barking in her crate. What should I do?

If you have an older dog that is barking in her crate, something has gone wrong with the training. Have you been consistent in your expectations? If not, now is the time to start. Did you crate train your dog for a few months when she was younger and then slack off the training? If so, you'll need to start from square one.

Reconditioning an older dog is much tougher than conditioning a puppy, but you can have some success by making her experience in the crate as pleasant as possible. An older dog that isn't used to being in a crate will become anxious and want to escape when confined to a crate. You'll need to accustom her to it gradually, taking the same steps as you would with a puppy. Leave some treats in the crate for her to enjoy when she enters. Feed her in the crate. Give her a chew toy in her crate. Make the crate a place where good things happen, and over the course of a few weeks her resistance will decrease.

Develop a command that tells her you want her to go to her crate. Leaving the crate open lures her into the crate. Reward her by marking the behavior and giving her a piece of food. Eventually, she'll become comfortable in her crate.

Sometimes people ask this question because they've been given an ultimatum by the neighbors or the landlord. The dog is barking, and they need a way to stop the noise immediately. If that's your situation, the answer is that you should have crate trained your dog. You'll have to use an electronic bark collar, which is effective but more stressful then crate training from the beginning. The collar has a sensor that picks up the vibration of the dog's neck when she barks, and emits an electronic correction. The longer and louder the dog barks, the stronger the correction becomes.

Though effective, this is a harsh and abrupt way to train your dog, and totally unnecessary if you crate train her from an early age. But if you're in a situation where you need to stop her barking very quickly, it may be your only option.

How do I stop my dog from pulling on her leash?

A majority of the time, a dog that pulls on her leash has never learned to walk calmly on a leash with a flat collar, and her owner is using a harness instead. If you're using a harness, your dog will certainly pull, because harnesses are designed to encourage pulling.

Many people default to a harness because the dog is choking herself when taken out on a leash. They don't want the dog to choke, so they resort to a harness. You fix the choking problem but simultaneously encourage the pulling behavior. To remedy this problem, you'll need to go back over the information in this book where we start phasing out the harness. Buy a flat collar, and start using it in conjunction with your harness. Then consider moving on to a flat collar in conjunction with a prong collar.

My dog keeps barking. What can I do to make her stop?

Try to understand why your dog is barking. If your dog is following you around and barking because she wants your attention, that's a very different situation from jumping up on the couch and barking at people she can see through the window.

In either case, however, the more freedom your dog has, the more likely she is to find a reason to bark. A crate trained dog will be in her crate when you can't give her 100 percent of your attention, so she won't be exposed to the triggers that stimulate her to start barking.

Whatever the specific problem, the solution is to take more control of the situation. If your dog's jumping on the back of the couch, put her in her crate, or prop something on the back of the couch so she can't get up there. Cut off the stimulation and you'll begin to eliminate the problem. Give her more exercise so she will be appropriately stimulated. This also has the advantage of tiring your dog out, making her more docile and receptive to being in her crate. Play tug with her. Do some obedience training. Take her to the park. When you're finished, she'll be ready to rest. A tired dog is less likely to bark.

Mental stimulation is important, too. Do some marker training to stimulate her brain. Teach her how to sit, roll over, beg, give you her paw. If you notice that your dog barks regularly at the same time of day, that's a good time to set aside for training. She's already worked up and motivated. It's a matter of redirecting her towards something constructive. Again, if you absolutely *must* stop the barking immediately, you can use an electronic bark collar, but this is a last resort.

My dog keeps using my home as a bathroom. How can I stop her?

Something has gone wrong with the crate training or the bathroom training process, and you're in a reactive position, rather than a proactive one.

This often occurs with dogs between six and fifteen months old. Their owners crate train them for a couple of months and then abandon the crate. The dog isn't properly housebroken yet, and when she gets the run of the house, she responds by going to the bathroom wherever she likes.

In that case, come up with a regular crate schedule. Involve everyone in the household, and make it very clear, so that the dog's movements are regulated whenever she's out of the crate. Without controls, younger dogs will naturally go to the bathroom anywhere they choose. With an older dog, focus on the times when your dog is having accidents, and control her freedom at those times.

Another factor may be water intake. Dogs will often drink well beyond the point of hydration. Consider controlling your dog's water intake by keeping her water dish empty and filling it from a jug when you want her to drink. Make sure that, if you do go down this route, she's getting enough water, particularly in summer. Check that you're using a high quality dog food, and giving her an appropriate quantity. Control her feeding times, and you'll be able to predict her bowel movements.

There is also a behavior called submissive urination. This is when a dog urinates to defuse any tension between her and whomever she might be peeing next to. Don't correct this behavior. Either ignore it entirely or redirect her attention with food and a lure. Engage her for thirty seconds or so. If her drive for the food is relatively high, this problem will go away, but you must be consistent.

How can I get my dog to stop chewing everything in sight?

Remove everything from sight. This is a simple case of managing your dog's movements. If she's always chewing on things, keep a tidy house and limit your dog's access to things she may want to chew. Make sure she has a couple of chew toys she can use to exercise her teeth.

If you're in the room while your dog is chewing, you aren't giving her 100 percent of your attention. Play some games with her, do some training, or return her to her crate. A well-managed dog won't encounter these issues, so consider how you can improve your management of your dog. Corrections can rectify the behavior, but can also create problems when done inappropriately.

How do I get my dog to stop digging up grass, flowerbeds and earth at every chance she gets?

Dogs will often dig because they have nothing better to do. If you let your dog outside to the backyard and leave her unattended for fifteen or twenty minutes, she may well start to dig. To prevent her, you need to find a more proactive way of exercising your dog. Take her for a walk or to a park for a game of fetch. Give her something more interesting to do than digging, and she'll redirect automatically.

Alternatively, there are yard-specific toys available, such as large plastic balls. These can attract your dog's attention and reduce the chances that she'll resort to digging. If keeping her out in the yard is essential, consider investing in a dig-proof environment. Create a playpen of an appropriate size, and use concrete for the floor. In extreme circumstances, you can rip up the grass and replace it with mulch.

Digging behavior can be corrected using an electric collar, provided that your dog understands the dynamics of the collar and has a solid training foundation. It's very important that your dog knows why she's being corrected, otherwise she may become anxious and confused.

My dog loves/hates being in the car and her behavior is annoying. What can I do?

Consider that your dog may be suffering from carsickness. If she is, consult your vet and get her some appropriate medication. You can't train dogs out of carsickness.

From a behavioral standpoint, this is tricky. An anxious dog in the car is annoying for the owner, but the dog is in a far worse condition, massively over-stimulated, confused, and anxious. The best way to calm a dog in a car is to crate her and reduce the stimulation. Some people allow their dogs to run free in the car, and that's a terrible idea. It's a big world, and the movement of the vehicle combined with the ever-changing view out the window will cause them to become far too stimulated. It's also dangerous, because there's nothing to prevent the dog from jumping onto the driver's lap or otherwise distracting the driver while the car is moving.

Unfortunately, a dog that's not comfortable being crated will be almost as stressed and anxious inside a crate as she will be running free in the car. The only true solution is to work on conditioning the dog to traveling in a crate. If your dog is a puppy, this should be part of her training anyway. For an older dog, you'll need to provide as many positive experiences as possible in the crate. Take a KONG full of peanut butter and throw it into the back of the crate for her. Give her a toy she can play with in the crate. Feed her in the crate. It will take a few weeks or months before your dog is totally calm and collected in her crate. At that point, you can start to take her in the car in her crate and expect her to be reasonably comfortable.

Consider throwing a blanket over the crate to reduce the stimulation levels for your dog. The smaller you can make her world, the easier it will be for her to relax. Don't try to use corrections to remedy this problem. Unless you're extremely skilled, you'll only make it worse.

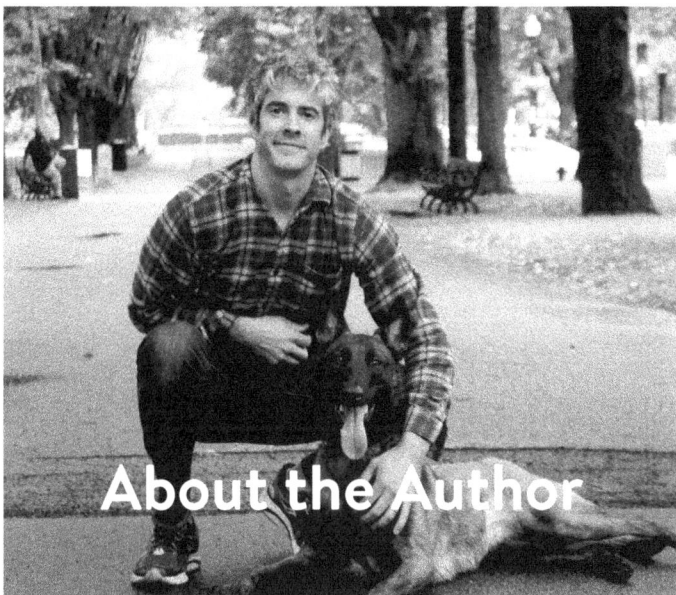

About the Author

With a lifelong love for dogs, Tom Roderick initially pursued his passion by working for a prestigious protection dog company in northern Massachusetts. It was there, as a senior trainer, that Tom trained and delivered obedience and protection dogs to clientele worldwide and developed a unique expertise for training dogs.

In 2010 he founded WalkyWalk and began his mission to mold dog owners into dog trainers. Since then he has established a large and loyal clientele across the Greater Boston area, and helped hundreds of dogs and owners be happy.

www.ingramcontent.com/pod-product-compliance
Lightning Source LLC
Chambersburg PA
CBHW071854020426
42331CB00010B/2509